CATCHING THE CONSCIENCE

CATCHING THE CONSCIENCE

Horton Davies

CAMBRIDGE, MASSACHUSETTS

International Standard Book No.: 0-936384-21-2
Library of Congress Catalog No.: 84-71181

Published in the United States of America by Cowley Publications.
Cover design by James Madden, SSJE.

To Marie - Helene

my wife and companion

in the correlation of theology and literature

with admiration and affection

ACKNOWLEDGMENTS

It is a pleasure for me to acknowledge the assistance of my editor, whose keen eye has detected and removed several blemishes in the style and expression of this book. I am grateful to Cynthia Shattuck for this rigorous help. Also, my wife, Dr. Marie-Helene Davies, has been most helpful in the research needed for these essays, and I value her constant encouragement. Finally, I wish to thank the several hundred students who through the years have attended the course I taught at Princeton University on "Religion and Modern Fiction," and whose insights have contributed to my understanding.

The following articles, since revised, are incorporated into the chapters that make up this book: "Gerard Manley Hopkins: The Self-Caged Skylark" (*Religion and Life,* Autumn 1970), "The God of Storm and Stillness: The Fiction of Flannery O'Connor and Frederick Buechner" (*Religion and Life,* Summer 1979), "Frederick Buechner and the Strange Work of Grace" (*Theology Today,* Summer 1979), and "Anagogical Signals in Flannery O'Connor's Fiction" (*Thought,* December 1982). I am grateful to the editors of these periodicals for the permission to reprint.

Horton Davies
Princeton University

CONTENTS

INTRODUCTION

Catching the Conscience

In *Hamlet* the tragic hero is determined to unmask the present king of Denmark, whom he suspects is the murderer of his father, the previous king. Hamlet, prince of Denmark, arranges for a group of court actors to represent on stage the scene of a poisoning, and offers as justification for this ruse,

> I have heard,
> That guilty creatures, sitting at a play,
> Have by the very cunning of the scene
> Been struck so to the soul that presently
> They have proclaim'd their malefactions;
> For murder, though it have no tongue, will speak
> With most miraculous organ.

In consequence, says Hamlet, "the play's the thing/ Wherein I'll catch the conscience of the king."

"Catching the conscience" has many artistic precedents for enticing the audience from its narrow, diurnal, stereotyped view to a more compassionate and reflective understanding of life. There are strong Biblical and novelistic precedents for such a procedure. For example, the prophet Nahum tells King David the story of the tyrant who killed the pet ewe lamb of a poor man (meaning Bathsheba stolen by David himself from Uriah), evoking from David the passionate outburst, "As the Lord lives, the man who did this deserves to die." The prophet then says to David, "You are the man" (2 Sam. 12:7). Jesus himself used a parable to illustrate compassion in the renowned story of the Good Samaritan. All the authors we consider in this book use their imagination as a decoy to shock us into seeing either the myopic nature of our customary vision—our narrow view through the distorting lenses of class or race or culture—or they provide the emancipated theological vision in which we see all are made in the image of God.

Graham Greene in his novel *The Power and the Glory* shows us that even religion can be used selfishly, as if one desired an exclusive telephone wire to God that is unlisted. Perhaps the finest sentence in the novel is when Greene enables his priest to see that "hatred is a failure of the imagination." A gifted novelist will enable us to make that discovery again and again. Another Roman Catholic novelist, François Mauriac, shows the anti-heroine, Brigitte Pian, using her apparent generosity to a poor couple only to make them totally subservient to her. On the other hand, the Anglican poet and novelist, Charles Williams, while illustrating the demonic manipulation of others by Simon the Clerk, in his novel *All Hallows' Eve*, also demonstrates how his heroine bears the terrible burden of another in a "substitution" which is modelled on that of Christ on the cross.

Albert Camus, who was not a Christian, diagnoses in *The Plague* the disease of egocentricity that makes almost everyone in Oran think first of escape rather than fighting the disease as members of a sanitary corps. Through the diary of a physician, Dr. Rieux, Camus documents the individual and corporate reaction to the bubonic plague: the escapes provided by extravagant expenditure or theatre-going, turnings towards faith, attempts at illegal escape, and finally the learning of the apprenticeship of solidarity in suffering. *The Plague* is also an allegory foretelling the growing evils of our society—the nuclear race towards annihilation, the increasing dominance of the State over private lives, and the growth of irresponsible and unassailable bureaucracy.

This psycho-drama is found in every author who lays bare the mixed motives of human beings. William Golding does this in his novel *The Spire* as he analyses the character of the fourteenth century dean of Salisbury Cathedral, who builds the tallest spire in England partly for the glory of God and partly for his own glory.

D.H. Lawrence, too, was eager to persuade Christians that they had become gnostics and dualists in their misprision of the body. It was as if they wished, Lawrence thought, to become bodiless spirits like angels before they had become real flesh and blood humans. This, to his view, seemed a curious misunderstanding on the part of adherents of a religion maintaining that God himself had taken human flesh in the Incarnation. His novel, *Sons and Lovers*, demonstrates the failure of the love between two characters, Paul and Miriam, because it is too platonic: "If people marry, they must live together as affectionate human beings, not as two souls." Christianity, supremely a religion of love and joy, had, so Lawrence claimed, degenerated into a morbid, censorious, life-denying legalism.

Thus the most compelling writers are as concerned as Hamlet was to see that their readers "have by the very cunning of the scene, been struck to the soul." The vividness of their imaginations is backed by the cleverness and diversity of their literary techniques.

Flannery O'Connor, the Roman Catholic writer of novels and short stories, catches our immediate attention by the very oddity and grotesqueness of her characters. For example, she exhibits the immaturity of a school teacher by her wearing girl-scout shoes, and she shows the conversion of Parker through his receiving of a tattoo of Jesus on his back, which he displays in the pool hall. But, lest we write off these characters as merely Southern eccentrics, she provides us with a series of anagogical signals, which will enable us to interpret the higher theological significance of her work. These include liturgical color symbolism and formulaic clues, which I will discuss in my essay on her short stories. Moreover, O'Connor demonstrates that God's providence is revealed in ordinary crises rather than in miraculous events. Unlike some Catholic novelists, she does not strain belief by intrusive supernatural incursions.

The Jesuit poet Gerard Manley Hopkins invented the new metric technique of sprung rhythm, and attempts to catch our

attention by his alliterative repetitions. By the exactitude of his
depiction of nature, or of the nuns facing death courageously in
"The Wreck of the Deutschland," Hopkins will glorify God as
creator and redeemer. Such masterly details etch the created
world vividly on the retina of the memory, as when the driven
snow is imaged as "wiry and white fiery and whirlwind swivelled
snow." No one can tell us as vividly and concisely of the impact
of Christ's incarnation as Hopkins does, himself made in the image
of God:

> In a flash, at a trumpet crash
> I am all at once what Christ is since he was what
> I am, and
> This jack, joke, poor potsherd, patch, matchwood
> Immortal diamond,
> Is immortal diamond.

Suppose that we have strong theological prejudices, and like
superior liberals, we insist that fundamentalists are to be explained
as finding the "fun" in "damning the mental," what we need is
the superb empathy of that gifted Presbyterian minister and
novelist Frederick Buechner. He will enable us to get beneath the
skin of a character like Leo Bebb, the Floridian evangelist, who
seems to be only a trickster and ex-prisoner selling ordination
certificates at five dollars each. Finally, like Antonio, a Northern
college graduate, who comes to Florida to expose Bebb, we will
recognize Bebb as an impressive servant of Christ. As the regional
and social scales of snobbery fall off Antonio's eyes, they disappear from our own. Thus we have been tricked into compassionate understanding, as we read the tetralogy of *The Book of
Bebb.*

By now it will be clear that our writers, with the exception of
the humanist Camus, have a double vocation—to religion and to
literature. The struggle between the two callings is not for most
of them as acute as it was for Gerard Manley Hopkins, who could
only reconcile himself to being a poet if his poems were hymns of

praise to God. He felt that poetry was a vocational distraction and that it led to thoughts of vainglory, glorifying the role of the senses rather than that of the will or the mind. Poetry could be redeemed only as returning gratitude to God who is "Beauty's self, Beauty's Giver."

Frederick Buechner is also an ordained minister, and his novels provide him with a wider pulpit than any local church could. This too has created difficulties. M.–H. Davies refers in her study of Buechner to "the tension Buechner feels as a man who is both a Christian and an artist, with the minister opposing the litterateur." For verisimilitude, a novelist must describe temptations as magnetic attractions, which counters his vocation as theologian. Buechner's novels seem to fall between two stools; the religious find his descriptions of evil too vivid, and secular folk find the novels too intrusively theological in character. Buechner, however, has as compensation a lively sense of humor in his theological novels which indicates both compassion and a sense of proportion. Wisdom and wit are closely allied, as may be seen in his translation of the saying of Jesus, "It is easier for a camel to pass through the eye of a needle than for a rich man to enter the kingdom of heaven." This Buechner modernizes as "easier for Nelson Rockefeller to pass through the night deposit slot of the Chase Manhattan Bank."

It is harder to create convincing saints in the making than to describe credible sinners. For this reason the eschatological fantasies of C.S. Lewis and Charles Williams avoid the need for credibility, which the down-to-earth novels of Greene, Mauriac, Golding and Buechner demand. All our writers, however, avoid the pitfalls of mediocre religious novels. Such novels include unimaginative propaganda and the creation of impossible Christ-figures—mere ghosts rather than living, breathing, flesh and blood figures.

The very credibility of the characters and situations imagined by our authors, furthermore, show that they have adopted the

rich insight of St. Paul contained in his second letter to the
Corinthians, where he states that the treasure of the Gospel is
found in earthen vessels. The New English Bible translates the
Greek thus: "We are no better than pots of earthenware to contain
this treasure, and this proves that such transcendent power does
not come from us, but is God's alone." If God's witnesses were
perfect, then the attention of the world would be focused merely
on the ambassadors of Christ and not on the king of kings whom
they represent.

That is why the clerical characters to whom we are introduced
may shock us at first by their inadequacy to their calling. Here
one thinks not only of Bebb, Buechner's initially improbable hero,
but even of the man whose life Bebb saves, Brownie, who always
sentimentalizes the sternest sayings of Jesus. Another example is
Greene's tippling priest in *The Power and the Glory*, who has
fathered an illegitimate child and yet who finally faces death in a
Marxist region of Mexico, where Catholicism has been prohibited.
He is a credible witness to God. The witness is all the more
impressive because it is plainly not of human achievement, but the
empowerment of the Holy Spirit. We find it initially shocking
that such are God's servants only because we confuse conventional
bourgeois virtue with the Christian life. We are natural Pelagians
who expect God's witnesses to be capable of pulling themselves
up by their own bootstraps, like the wooden martyr whose improbable hagiography the Mexican mother is reading to her boy
as the novel ends.

Mauriac, too, shows us a priest who becomes all the more
God's servant after he had been for a time forbidden to celebrate
the Mass. The priest's intellectual pride and disdain for the female
Pharisee have narrowed his own vision, and he must be humbled.
It is this new humility which enables the priest finally to win
Brigitte Pian, the proud rich pietist, for Christ.

Robert Burns, the shrewed Scottish poet, prayed

O wad som Pow'r the giftie gie us,
To see oursels as others see us.
It wad frae mony a blunder free us
And foolish notion

and it is such mirrors that the novelistic critics of Christianity are delighted to supply us with. In *The Plague* Camus presents us with the Jesuit Father Paneloux, who apparently knows all the answers to life's problems. To a full cathedral congregation, gathered for High Mass after the plague has broken out, he preaches a sermon declaring that the plague is sent by God in judgement on the flagrant sins of the citizens. The remedy is repentance. Much later at a second service, when the cathedral is half empty, his approach is much humbler. He now claims that difficult as it is, one has to assert the role of God in all events, for the Almighty is all or nothing. Finally, in a scene reminiscent of Dostoyevsky's *The Brothers Karamazov*, as a child is tortured through the last night of his anguished life by the plague, Paneloux's faith is also tormented. He joins the risky band of the healers, and ultimately he dies, clutching a crucifix—his last statement of faith. He who originally believed in viewing life from the safety of the balcony has now gone down into the arena and become part of a compassionate commitment to the human struggle.

The three critics of the church to whom we devote the final essay are Somerset Maugham, Sinclair Lewis and the witty Peter De Vries. The first two are unbelievers, while the third delivers the wounds of a friend.

Somerset Maugham presents in weaker form the Freudian view of Christianity as a human projection, born out of fear of developing into maturity and of the cut-throat competition of life and, especially, the terror of death. It is based on the incapacity to face the fact that humans are all orphans in the universe. Hence in the story "Rain" Maugham's medical missionary, Doctor

Davidson, is depicted as a sexually repressed individual who
commits adultery with a prostitute he is supposedly converting
to Christianity. Ultimately he commits suicide, proving thereby
that his life was an illusion based upon an unacceptable religion.
The usual clinical objectivity of the medically trained Maugham
is totally rejected when he deals with Christian characters in his
short-stories, plays, or novels. The free-thinker is anything but
free in his prejudices. This we see in his autobiographical novel
Of Human Bondage, where Maugham satirizes the meanness,
the manipulativeness, and the mediocrity of the Vicar of Blackstable.

The Marxist critique of religion also regards Christianity as
an illusion, but views the institutional Church as sanctifying the
economic status quo of the have-nots by promising them "pie in
the sky when you die." Despite Christianity's claim to create
brotherhood, it has, says the Marxist, stratified class, national,
and ethnic divisions. Less a Marxist than an old-fashioned Socialist, Sinclair Lewis sees Jesus as comrade carpenter in his novel
The Carpenter, and he directs his criticism against the individualism of the revivalistic pietists of his day who believed in a
futuristic "O it will be, Glory for me" type of faith. His *Elmer
Gantry* makes one rightly suspicious of evangelistic techniques
which encourage orgies of emotionalism, manipulate the crowd,
and use fake statistics.

The third critic of the contemporary Church is Peter De Vries.
He condemns extremist theologies both of the right and of the
left. He satirizes fundamentalism because it disallows reason, and
extreme liberalism, because it destroys Christian discipleship.
His literary barbs are chiefly directed at the snobbishness which
turns a commuters' suburban church into a club, and his witty
explosion is concentrated in the novel *The Mackerel Plaza*. But
the fundamentalists are not ignored: to a street-corner evangelist
who asked, "Brother, have you found Christ?", the Rev. Mr. Mackerel answers: "What? Is he lost again?"

Closing line

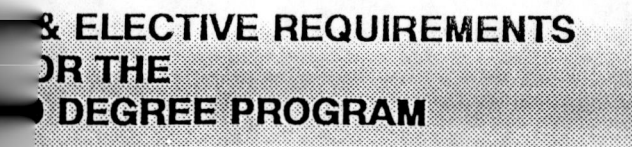

& ELECTIVE REQUIREMENTS
OR THE
DEGREE PROGRAM

- Other course possibilities:
  * Astronomy   * Zoology
  * Geology   * Botany
  * Oceanography   * Anatomy
  * Nutrition   * Physiology

UDE ADP 335)

- Sociology
- Political Science
- Geography

can)

Maybe it is because Christ seems absent from the modern world picture that the Church needs its novelists, both critical and constructive, to help to correlate the Christian faith with contemporary life.

GERARD MANLEY HOPKINS

The Self-Caged Skylark

The life of Gerard Manley Hopkins, the Jesuit poet, is one of fascinating obscurity from which his incandescent poems emerge like fireworks in a fog of mystery. He was born in 1844 and died in 1889, but his poems were not published until 1918 by Robert Bridges, England's poet laureate and author of *The Testament of Beauty*. From time to time we have tantalizing glimpses of him, but each glimpse seems to pose a problem of interpretation. Why, for example, did Hopkins prefer painting to poetry as a schoolboy at Highgate grammar school? It is, of course, entirely understandable that with his mosaic love of detail, his sense of "inscape" or patterning, and above all his prolific and powerful visual imagination, he should have liked painting. We can even imagine that he might, to the loss of poetry, have become another Rossetti, Burne Jones, or even a Holman Hunt. But the query remains: What caused Hopkins to turn from painting to poetry? The curtain of obscurity drops again.

We find him next at Balliol College, Oxford, at a time when the influence of the Oxford movement was fading and the Liberal churchmen were in the ascendancy. Benjamin Jowett, the iconoclast, was a don of Balliol and Matthew Arnold, who defined religion in a most untheological way as "morality touched with emotion," was professor of poetry in the University. Here, while presumably preparing for the ordained ministry of the Church of England, with the future before him, Hopkins suddenly at the age of twenty-two joined the Roman Catholic Church, and two years later entered the ranks of the Society of Jesus. Why? Next, we hear of him as an ordained Jesuit priest working among Irish immigrants in the Liverpool slums, without any great reputation as a preacher. This is again curious for such a great wordsmith, so readily moved to compassion and full of devotion to his Lord.

The darkness falls again, and then lifts, only to reveal him teaching classics at Stonyhurst College in Lancashire.

At the age of forty, Hopkins became professor of Greek at
University College in Dublin. Five years later he was dead, killed
by typhoid fever, on June 8, 1889. Then, perhaps the most
remarkable thing of all, his friend Robert Bridges, poet laureate
of England, feeling that Hopkins' poetry was too far in advance of
Victorian and Edwardian taste and technique with its telegraphic
brevity and obscurity, its jerking "sprung rhythm," and its passionate religious profundity, kept it hidden and released it only in
1918—twenty-nine years after the poet's death. So Hopkins's very
reputation is a resurrection, a postmortem fame!

In my own approach to Hopkins I hope to illuminate his
poetry by the consideration of a central vocational dilemma, or
paradox, that this brilliant religious poet was an exceedingly reluctant writer of poetry. I would like to examine the evidence for
my conviction that poetry posed a conflict for Hopkins, and consider the reasons for the conflict. Then I would like to look at
how he overcame this reluctance and finally persuaded himself
that he could glorify God in poetry.

From the outset I dismiss as entirely unsatisfactory explana-
tions of this reluctance to write poetry which claim that Hopkins,
despite the greatness of the urge and the talent, was a lazy man
with an infinite gift for postponement. I also reject the notion
that this classical scholar, with his exquisite appreciation of sense
and sound in words and of the best way to arrange them for
alliteration, assonance, and rhythmic effect, was such a perfectionist that he was paralyzed by his own ideals. The Jesuit order was
not designed by St. Ignatius Loyola to afford its members super-
annuated leisure; it is an order of men actively devoted to preaching and teaching, and ruled by the firmest of disciplines. Thus,
Hopkins, far from having illimitable time for writing poetry, was

more likely to have found himself too tired by the end of the day to welcome the opportunity. Perfectionist he undoubtedly was, but perfectionism did not prevent him from writing sermons, nor, when his conscience permitted, from writing the first drafts of poems. Perfectionism may have delayed the completion of his poems, but it did not destroy Hopkins's urge to write.

One theory that tries to account for the paradox of the reluctant poet has been fully expounded by another Jesuit, Fr. Chester Burns, in an essay entitled "Gerard Manley Hopkins, Poet of Ascetic and Aesthetic Conflict." His view is that Hopkins felt no inherent conflict between the demands of his religious order and the writing of poetry, but that there was simply a powerful collision in a sensitive mind between duty and delight. It is Burns's opinion that the conscience of the man of religion was reluctant, unless bidden by a superior of the society, to spend time on poetry that should be spent on glorifying God through worship or contemplation or on instruction in the faith. From this viewpoint, Hopkins simply made a difficult pragmatic decision: to keep for religion the time he took away from writing poetry. Fr. Burns rightly insists that a religious order "is not a society consecrated to the dainty worship of aesthetic sanctities" (though such a description seems to view the good red steak of Hopkins as if it were *pâté de foie gras*, and hardly does justice to the vigor and the religious power of his poems) and that such "an organization of rugged purpose seriously bent on serving God as its proper constitutions require" does not allow time or opportunity for cultivating the fancy. Such a statement does, however, ignore the fact that a distinguished Elizabethan poet, Robert Southwell, the author of a superb lyric of metaphysical quality in honor of the Incarnation, "The Burning Babe," was able to combine asceticism and aestheticism as a Jesuit. My chief complaint against Burns's well-argued essay is that it oversimplifies the nature of the problem as largely and almost entirely a matter of Hopkins's chronic shortage of time. I will contend that it was a multifaceted decision, of which one important facet was a conscience about spending time on poetry that ought to be spent on God's work.

Fr. Burns rightly finds support for his own contention in these words from a letter of 5 October 1878 written by the poet to a friend, the Rev. R.W. Dixon, who had appealed to him not to waste his poetic gifts: "I cannot find it in my conscience to spend time on [poetry]." Three years later, in a letter of November 2, 1881, he gives the same friend a list of his regrets, thus: "For the backward glances I have given with my hand upon the plough, for the waste of time the very compositions you admire may have caused and their preoccupation of the mind which belonged to more sacred or more binding duties, for the disquiet and thoughts of vainglory they have given rise to."

At the end of the second letter we have a very significant clue which Fr. Burns has not followed up; for Hopkins, the writing of poetry gave rise to thoughts of vainglory. The personal art of writing poetry was far more than a distraction from a religious vocation; it took away from the greater glory of God to which the Society of Jesus is dedicated, and put in its place the self-glorification of the author. It was a task that might lead to that fame which another religious poet, John Milton, has called "that last infirmity of noble mind." Hopkins belonged to a religious order that attempted in the most rigorous fashion to cultivate such an obedience to Christ that all egotism was burnt out of the soul. Its cultivation of "cadaveric" obedience was intended to uproot the very flowers of the vanity which Gerard Manley Hopkins was cultivating by writing poetry. In the best religious orders there is a disciplined anonymity in the corporate work done for God. What can be less corporate and more individual, less predictable and undisciplined, than the poetic inspiration? This, I believe, was the subtlest of all temptations that this intensely spiritual man faced.

I think it was all the subtler for him because he had not gained the popularity of some of the great Jesuit preachers, despite the fact that his gifts were no less impressive than theirs. Nor did he, like his mentor, John Henry Newman, have an admiring group of disciples who joined in the creed, *Credo in unum Newmanum*, though Hopkins was a teacher at college and university. Newman had written the hymn "Lead, Kindly Light" and the religious poem "The Dream of Gerontius"; there, at least, was a safe example in a preeminent servant of God. Might not Hopkins get a decent satisfaction and acclaim from the appearance of his name at the end of a few lyrics printed in elegant anthologies? Surely, here was no titanic or towering ambition, but only a lonely and sensitive man's longing for a little appreciation. Yet Hopkins knew it is from such apparently innocent roots that the strangling weeds of pride are grown. In writing to Dixon he indicates how fully aware he was of the spiritual danger attendant upon the fame that publication of his poems might bring him:

> The question for me is not whether I am willing . . .
> to make a sacrifice of hopes of fame (let us suppose), but
> whether I am not to undergo a severe judgment from God
> for the lothness I have shewn in making it . . . for the
> backward glances I have given with my hand upon the
> plough, for the waste of time the very compositions you
> admire may have caused, for the thoughts of vainglory
> they have given rise to.

How, then, did Hopkins overcome these scruples? Quite simply, I believe, in two ways. In the first case the decision was made for him. His initial silence of seven years in the Jesuit Order was ended by the suggestion of a superior that he ought to commemorate in a poem the splendid and heroic faith of five Franciscan nuns who died at sea in 1875. From this occasion came Hopkins's poem, "The Wreck of the Deutschland." This suggestion fully overcame his scruples. A deeper explanation, I believe, is that Hopkins came to see that he could glorify God in poetry by writing what were, in effect, highly personal and idiosyncratic *hymns*. A hymn is, after all, a poetic composition addressed to God. It is surely very significant that Hopkins's major poems are strong in theological references and even directly address divine persons. "The Windhover," which uses the image of a falcon riding the skies like a horseman as an image for Christ, is not only

dedicated "to Christ our Lord," but addresses him directly as
"O my chevalier!" "The Blessed Virgin Compared to the Air We
Breathe" leads Hopkins to delight in recalling "God's infinity,
Dwindled to infancy" in its marvelous condescension and in
rebirths in the spirit, creating" . . . O marvellous! New Nazareths
in us" only to conclude,

> Be thou then, O thou dear
> Mother, my atmosphere. . . .
> Wound with thee, in thee isled,
> Fold home, fast fold thy child.

"The Wreck of the Deutschland" begins, like one of John Donne's
sonnets, with a direct address to God:

> THOU mastering me
> God! giver of breath and bread;
> World's strand, sway of the sea;
> Lord of living and dead;
> Thou hast bound bones and veins in me, fastened me flesh
> And after it almost unmade, what with dread,
> Thy doing: and dost thou touch me afresh?
> Over again I feel thy finger and find thee.

One might notice in this poem the high Ignatian emphasis on
obedience to God and the adoration of the true disciple.

> Be adored among men,
> God, three-numberèd form;
> Wring thy rebel, dogged in den,
> Man's malice, with wrecking and storm.
> Beyond saying sweet, past telling of tongue,
> Thou art lightning and love, I found it, a winter and warm . . . .

> With an anvil-ding
> And with fire in him forge thy will

Or rather, rather then, stealing as Spring
Through him, melt him but master him still:
Whether at once, as once at a crash Paul,
Or as Austin, a lingering-out swéet skill,
    Make mercy in all of us, out of us all
Mastery, but be adored, but be adored King.

This is clearly a passionate hymn or poetic prayer addressed to
God. But the religious intensity achieved in "The Wreck of the
Deutschland" is to be found even in a poem that could easily be
included in an anthology of nature poems, "Pied Beauty," that
superb catalog of 'dappled things.' This poem to nature begins:
"GLORY be to God for dappled things" and ends, "Praise Him."
This opening and closing, and the theological ring that echoes in
all his poems, convince me that it was because Hopkins regarded
his poetry not only as religious poetry, but as *hymnody*, and that
in attempting to satisfy a critic more demanding than R.W. Dixon
or Robert Bridges—namely, Christ himself—he was able to overcome his scruples. He would then be writing hymns not to
glorify himself but to glorify God, and even a busy Jesuit priest
might be permitted to write of his ecstatic joy in God. A humanistic poetry would not do; instead, Hopkins became a lyrical,
rhapsodic hymnodist, Gerard the Hymnographer.

    Hopkins saw the writing of poetry as potentially, we have
seen, a dereliction of primary duty, but even more as a dangerous
temptation to egotism. But implicit in the poetic art there lay a
third trap, the danger that the poet might commit the sin of
idolatry in loving the created order in lieu of its Creator, glorying
in the ever-fresh splendor of dawn or the grandeur of the sunset
instead of in the divine artist whose palette is the cosmos. This
kind of idolatry is the peculiar temptation of the artist with a
visual imagination and a careful recording eye for detail; so it was
in a large measure the special temptation of Gerard Manley

Hopkins, whose poetry abounds in the masterly details that linger
on the retina of the mind. Nor was this an unconscious temptation for Hopkins; he knew only too well how the aesthetic fights
the ethical.

How could he guard against losing that transparency in the
viewing of nature which goes through nature to nature's God?
Fortunately for Hopkins there were two powerful religious influ-
ences on him which never allowed him to forget the doctrine of
creation. The first was that vivid devotional masterwork for
training priests in the likeness of their Lord, the *Spiritual Exercises* devised by Ignatius Loyola, founder of the Jesuits, a
devotional discipline that takes a month to complete. The
Exercises begin with an assertion of God's love for his creatures,
following a survey of the varied but continuing communication of
God in his visible creation. Indeed Hopkins expresses this well in
his *Commentary on the Exercises*: "God's utterance of himself
is this world. This world then is word, expression, news, of God.
Therefore its end, its purpose, its purport, its meaning is God, and
its life or work to name and praise him."

The other great influence on Hopkins's spirituality was the
medieval English Franciscan philosopher, Duns Scotus, whom he
studied in 1872 and in whose writings Hopkins discovered a
philosophical corroboration of his own private theory of individuation. Scotus asserted that the mind working through the senses
has a direct union with the individual concrete object, rather than
with a mere concept of a class or group. Each individual object
has its own special character, what Scotus called its *haecceitas*, its
"thusness." And this idea gave the poet a double sanction: first,
for the careful individual conservation of things, and second and
more personally, for asserting his individuality as a Christian poet.
It is significant that Thomas Aquinas, a philosopher greatly
admired by the Jesuits, was no nominalist but rather believed
that the mind has direct contact only with the universal concepts;
Aquinas held to a more abstract and less individuated truth. The
same St. Thomas, although he produced the greatest encyclopedia

of philosophy and faith, the *Summa Theologica*, said that all he
had written was only fit to be burned. Duns Scotus is described
by Hopkins in his poem, "Duns Scotus's Oxford," as "the one
who of all men most sways my spirits to peace;/Of reality the
rarest-veined traveller." True poetic creation occurred, according
to Hopkins, when his own nature corresponded to some complementary inscape found in external nature. It is this discovery
that rings all through his sonnet, "As Kingfishers Catch Fire."
Individuality and individuation in things and people are the faces
of God in them.

> For Christ plays in ten thousand places
> Lovely in limbs, and lovely in eyes not his
> To the Father through the features of men's
>   faces.

Hopkins explains in a letter of 24 September 1883 to the Catholic
poet, Coventry Patmore, his convictions on the revelatory power
of nature: "It is certain that in nature outward beauty is the
proof of inward beauty, outward good of inward good. Fineness,
proportion of feature comes from a moulding force which suc-
ceeds in asserting itself over the resistance of cumbersome or
restraining matter . . . The moulding force, the life, is the form in
the philosophical sense."

His *Journal* shows how clearly Hopkins saw through nature to
nature's God and thought God's thoughts after him. Here, for
example, is his comment on seeing the northern lights for the first
time: "The busy working of nature wholly independent of the
earth and seeming to go on in a strain of time not reckoned by our
reckoning of days and years, but simply as if correcting the preoccupation of the world by being preoccupied with and appealing to
and dated to the day of judgment, was like a new witness to God
and filled me with delightful fear." On another occasion the poet
records his observations: "As we drove home the stars came out
thick: I leant back to look at them and my heart opening more
than usual praised our Lord to whom and in whom all that beauty
comes home."

Such a conviction as St. Paul records in his letter to the Romans, that we ascend through the visible things of creation to the invisible God, strengthened by Duns Scotus, the Subtle Doctor, reinforced and justified by marvelous precision of observation, with the splendidly individualized descriptions of objects, gleamed in all his poetry. Shakespeare alone, one would hazard, had such a gift for forging vivid images, as the following selected catalog shows. For human beings alone on earth praise their creator, and how freshly minted are these descriptions of the infinite variety of created beauty: "the moon, dwindled and thinned to the fringe of fingernail held to the candle," "sheep-flock clouds like worlds of wool," "wiry and white-fiery and whirlwind swivelled snow," a river with its "wind-wandering, wild-winding bank," a stream as a "darksome burn, horseback brown," thrush's eggs resembling "little low heavens," and Oxford perfectly mirrored as "branchy between towers; cuckoo-echoing, bell-swarmèd, lark-charmèd, rook-racked, river-rounded; the dapple-eared lily below thee."

Perhaps this catalog of images and impressions would not have been possible had not Hopkins constantly remembered that God must always be acknowledged in his gifts. By recognizing and acknowledging distinctness in things and persons, Hopkins could thereby affirm the divine impress and character of every created thing, its dependence upon God. The aim of all true poetry is, as Hopkins writes in "The Golden Echo," "Give beauty back, beauty, beauty, beauty, back to God, beauty's self and beauty's giver."

There was also, I believe, a fourth reason for the poet's fundamental suspicion of the art and craft of writing poetry. The reason is that while art is the glorification of the senses, religion is the obedience of faith in the tamed will. Aestheticism can so easily lead to the utter dissolution of the will's determination. The practice of religion is not idle dreaming, creating new forms from the changing skyscape of the clouds or wandering like a darting kingfisher wherever the iris-freighted river leads. For a Jesuit in particular, it is the conformity of a disciplined will to the divine design and destiny.

The primacy of the will and the difficulty of bending the will is a common theme in Hopkins's poetry. In one of the "dark" sonnets, its is expressed thus:

> We hear our hearts grate on themselves: it kills
> To bruise them dearer. Yet the rebellious wills
> Of us we do bid God bend to him even so.

The poem entitled "Carrion Comfort," like Jacob at Jabbock, reveals that religion is a wrestling with God, fighting against God's "lionlimb." It is quite typical that the one psalm he translates and transposes into modern experience begins: "Thou art indeed just, Lord, if I contend/With thee; but, sir, what I plead is just." Why does Hopkins so greatly admire military men, writing poems on "The Bugler's First Communion" and "The Soldier?" It is surely because the soldier is par excellence a creature of obedience, as the Christian should be, and the Jesuit order is a military order founded by a soldier.

In a poem written when he was twenty-one or twenty-two, "The Habit of Perfection," Hopkins shows how powerfully aware he is of the seduction of the senses. He prays:

> Be shellèd, eyes, with double dark
> And find the uncreated light:
> This ruck and reel which you remark
> Coils, keeps, and teases simple sight.

Spare and simple diet best feeds the soul:

> Palate, the hutch of tasty lust,
> Desire not to be rinsed with wine:

The can must be so sweet, the crust
So fresh that come in fasts divine!

There are great compensations for the dedicated senses:

O feel-of-primrose hands, O feet
That want the yield of plushy sward,
But you shall walk the golden street
And you unhouse and house the Lord.

To read and, much more, to write poetry was always for
Hopkins a playing with fire—the fire of the unbridled imagination
that runs through the heavens like Phaeton's fabled coursers.
The twin dangers of benevolent sensualism and democratic compassion, as well as nature-mysticism, he saw expressed in the
poems of Walt Whitman, his contemporary in America. It is this
sense of danger which explains Hopkins's judgment of Whitman in
a letter to Robert Bridges: "I always knew in my heart Walt
Whitman's mind to be more like my own than any other man's
living. As he is a very great scoundrel, this is not a pleasant confession. And this also makes me the more desirous to read him and
the more determined that I will not." He may have seen Whitman
as his alter ego, the uninhibited sensual man of great goodwill to
all that Hopkins might have been if poetry had overcome his
religious vocation, if the senses triumphed over the will subordinated to God. It was Plato, the myth-making philosopher himself,
who had the wisdom to banish poets from his ideal republic.

How did Hopkins tame this last temptation? Just as he had
drawn the claws of the other three—by grace, by the perseverance
and self-discipline he had learned in the Society of Jesus, and by
making the slender body of his poems the mirror of a spirit
dedicated to the devoted discipleship of Christ. Hopkins was, in
the last analysis, not only a great poet of the natural world, although he was that, of course, and no English poet has more
radiantly seen that the world is charged with the grandeur of God,

like electricity or 'shook foil.' But he was, most profoundly, a *poet of grace*. And it was in this way that the callings of the poetic and the religious were fused, and he overcame his life's greatest dilemma and dualism.

Hopkins's greatest theme is the rebirth of grace, of how the Incarnation is continued as Christ is conceived and born in the human soul through grace a thousand times each day. Such a birth of grace took place in the tall nun in the foundering ship, the 'Deutschland.' Even though the "rash, smart, sloggering brine blinds her," she calls on her Master, "*Ipse*, the only one, Christ, King, Head"; and thus "the cross to her she calls Christ to her, christens her world-worst Best." Cooperating with the grace of God that came to her amidst the shipwreck, the nun gives birth once more to the fuller life of Christ within her soul. As a reward, "she has thee for the pain, for the patience."

Hopkins lets us see, especially in his greatest poem, "The Wreck of the Deutschland," how grace enables us to take the bitterness out of suffering and disappointment. He lets us see that this is possible only by linking our suffering with Christ's on the cross, by turning it into sacrifice. Like the suffering of the five nuns on the doomed ship who unite their lives to Christ, suffering can become reparative and redemptive for all men and women:

> Five! the finding and sake
> And cipher of suffering Christ.
> Mark, the mark is of man's make
> And the word of it Sacrificed.
> But he scores it in scarlet himself on his own bespoken
> Before-time-taken, dearest prizèd and priced.

Hopkins also knew that to suffer with Christ here on earth means to be triumphant with him hereafter. This is superb confidence that trumpets the last lines of "That Nature Is a Heraclitean Fire and of the comfort of the Resurrection":

                                          the Resurrection,
A heart's-clarion! Away grief's gasping, joyless days,
     dejection.
               Across my foundering deck shone
A beacon, an eternal beam. Flesh fade, and mortal trash
Fall to the residuary worm; world's wildfire, leave but ash:
          In a flash, at a trumpet crash,
I am all at once what Christ is, since he was what I am, and
This Jack, joke, poor potsherd, patch, matchwood,
     immortal diamond,
                    Is immortal diamond.

The reluctant poet overcame his reluctance only by producing
poems that were hymns, prayers, and creeds, wrought on his
knees. Unable to write poetry, he is the self-caged skylark. But
composing, he is a skylark daring the gales, wholly himself in his
own high azure atmosphere.

D. H. LAWRENCE

A Revaluation

Is David Herbert Lawrence also among the prophets? Is this adopted son of Sigmund Freud also among the saints? A revaluation of Lawrence's understanding of human life is surely long overdue when the distinguished literary critic, F.R. Leavis, has insisted that he cannot forgive the Christians for not recognizing that Lawrence was on their side, and the former Bishop of Woolwich, Dr. J.A.T. Robinson, has been reprimanded by his Archbishop for arguing that sex was as sacramental to Lawrence as Holy Communion to an Anglican.

At first glance it must be acknowledged that Lawrence is a very unlikely prospect as a Christian prophet, but so were Saul of Tarsus and Augustine of Hippo. More recently, C.S. Lewis has reminded us in *Surprised by Joy* that when he became convinced of the truth of Christianity on the top of a double-decker bus, he was the most sorry and reluctant convert in all England. Even with these exceptions in mind, Lawrence's Christian credentials look unpromising. By the general public he was thought to be a pornographer and a smut hound and the author of the foulest novel in English, *Lady Chatterley's Lover* (1928). This novel, for which Lawrence was tried in England on charges of obscenity, recounts the story of a woman whose husband, a mine owner in the north of England, is paralyzed from the waist down. She desires a child and for its father turns to her husband's gamekeeper; the story of their developing love is written in frank detail, with the greatest respect for the flowering of passion and the transformation it brings about in both of them. Nowhere is there the trace of the lewd leer of the peeping Tom-ism of the voyeur. And when Lawrence is accused of being an obscene novelist, his own noble essay on "Pornography and Obscenity" is entirely ignored, with its warning that "pornography is the attempt to insult sex, to do dirt on it. This is unpardonable." At considerable length Lawrence inveighs against the insult, arguing that pornography is insulting to the beauty of the human body, and the cheapening of a vital act of sexual tenderness which renders it "trivial, and cheap and nasty." It could be argued, indeed, that Lawrence is more easily identified as a Puritan than as a pornographer.

What are we to make of another common accusation, namely, that his is a fascistic doctrine of blood and soil? Certainly there is in Lawrence a snobbishness, a too facile disentanglement from the attitudes and values of the working men in the colliery town of his youth, which is clearly to be seen in his dislike of his coalminer father and his preference for his sensitive and cultured mother in the most autobiographical of the novels, *Sons and Lovers*. Furthermore, it is significant that between the first and third versions of *Lady Chatterley's Lover* Lawrence finds it necessary to make the character of Mellors the gamekeeper more sensitive and cultivated, as if these were qualities not easily discoverable in a man in that level of society. But granted that Lawrence acknowledged men and women's kinship with the soil and the animals, his only description of such a society, *The Plumed Serpent*, a transcript of his Mexican sojourn published in 1926, left him profoundly dissatisfied with it. Moreover, Lawrence advocates neither violence nor racism, so that the similarity of his views with those of the dictators, Mussolini and Hitler, the true fascists, is so superficial as to be negligible. In his novels Lawrence is so much more successful in depicting the middle classes, the intelligentsia, Bohemia, and the squirearchy (though not very sympathetic with the latter) than in rendering the working classes as three-dimensional characters, that one might suppose a failure of empathy. That failure, however, is far from being an indication of fascism.

A third and more serious charge to be brought against Lawrence is that of blasphemy. Here the critic has in mind Lawrence's heterodox study, *The Man Who Died* (1928). While the novelist does not mention Christ by name, the novella is

clearly an attempt to tell a revised story of the risen Christ's life
in the body. The claim is made that it is in the return from the
dead that Christ's second incarnation is fully, humanly, and
sexually in the body, and in the novel's climax Lawrence claims
that in the meeting and union with the priestess of Osiris the
fullness of that humanity is reached. Thus, in the strictest literal
sense, the proof of resurrection is erection.

From the standpoint of an orthodox Christian, this rewriting
of the return of the risen Christ is blasphemy. If we understand
Lawrence's intentions correctly, however, it is not. Lawrence is
referring to a mythical figure (for him) in Jesus, as mythical as
the priestess of Osiris. Furthermore the Christ-figure is seen
allegorically as the figure of Lawrence himself, and the point of
the story is not to diminish Christ but to use him as a symbol.
Here, Christ stands not for Christianity, but rather for the
abstracting and excessive spiritualizing of life itself to the loss of
the richness of the sensual. To suffer this loss is in Lawrence's
view to become a corpse and a ghost, without ever having been
fully a human being. Lawrence was looking in this novella for the
proper relationship between the spirituality of the Christian God
of light and the dark, chthonic, earthly, sensual powers of nature,
both of which are necessary to a balanced humanity, in
Lawrence's view. So although Lawrence can hardly be called an
orthodox Christian, his novel *The Man Who Died* can be read as
an allegory or parable of the balanced life, in which spirituality
and sense, the proper claims of soul and body, heaven and earth,
light and darkness, are balanced and united.

A fourth criticism leveled against Lawrence is that he is the
protagonist of a brand of romantic naturalism, or of what Aldous
Huxley has called "mystical materialism." It has been argued that
while one can find traces of pantheism in his accounts of the
strong kinship between human beings and nature, yet the sense of
wonder we find in Lawrence is wholly attributed by him to an
immanent source and not to a transcendent God. If this criticism
means that Lawrence, like the early Ernest Hemingway, attempted

to describe men as breathing, fighting, eating, lusting animals, without any trace of the image of God in them, an image either perfect or marred by original sin, this is partly true. But as Hemingway felt it was necessary to find some larger purpose for his 'stoical man,' so did Lawrence turn to a mystical faith in the values of blood and soil, of living close to the earth with passion. Like Hemingway, he fought against an arid, desiccated rationalism that has turned men and women into cerebral ghosts, mere gray matter, skeletal vestiges of their virile selves. Like Rousseau, he believed that the return to nature and the recovery of the full instinctual life of love that accompanies such a return would recreate humanity.

Lawrence was highly suspicious of the dissecting intellect. "My great religion," he writes, "is belief in the blood, the flesh, as being wiser than the intellect. We can go wrong in our minds. But what our flesh believes and says, is always true. The intellect is only a bit and a bridle." Lawrence feared not only the intellect as a divisive force, creating suspicions, as opposed to the unitive power of instinct; he also feared the tyrannical domination of the will, another great divider among human beings. He felt that human beings are united most profoundly in their instincts, and he believed that there is a deep kind of unreflective human consciousness that leads to contentment, whereas the reflective and discursive consciousness of the intellect was ever busy, ever agitating, ever dissatisfied. For this reason Lawrence was decried as an anti-intellectual, an irrationalist, and a Philistine in the Thirties and Forties, before the days of popular existentialism. The relationship between Lawrence's 'intuitionism' as a basis of unity, and Christianity's emphasis on the primacy of love as the nexus of human relationships, was simply not seen by Lawrence's critics. Furthermore, his novels may exalt the role of the instincts, but the novels themselves are very reflectively planned and developed. It can then be said that the charges that Lawrence is a pornographer, a fascist, a blasphemer, and an irrationalist are greatly exaggerated, if not wholly untrue.

What is perhaps far more exciting to consider is the impressive critique of the current expression of Christian thought and life that Lawrence offers in his novels and essays. It is only after we have examined these in some detail that we can come to a conclusion on the controversial question of whether Lawrence was a Christian or a pagan, or a combination of both.

It is certain that he was very critical of certain emphases in Christianity. His first and most frequently repeated criticism was that Christianity's understanding of the nature of God was far too moralistic and far too "spiritual." Lawrence criticized the Christian churches because their idea of God was too small. In particular, he attacked the notion of an all-powerful totalitarian deity operating a celestial C.I.A. bearing the device of a vast omniscient eye and the legend, "Thou God seest me." Those are, of course, my words but here are Lawrence's:

> The Catholic Church has fallen into the same disaster as
> the Protestant in preaching a moral God, instead of
> Almighty God, the God of strength, and glory, and might,
> and wisdom; a 'good God' instead of a vital and magnif-
> icent God . . . .

He makes a single exception to this condemnation. Only in the countryside among peasants, where the old ritual of the seasons holds sway, Lawrence believes, is there still a living and instinctive faith in the God of life. All the natural religions of mankind have stressed the creative fecundity of God, the fertility which is given to nature and to man, but this has become reduced and attenuated in Christianity to the point of disappearance. Moreover—and this is a powerful part of the same criticism—the God of Lawrence's Christian contemporaries has become too "spiritual." Now what does Lawrence mean by this apparent contradiction? He means that Christianity is like a dialogical seance with a ghost whispering to disembodied souls, instead of a religion that bows in awe and majesty before the creator of lightnings, whose voice is the rolling thunder and whose echo is heard in the cyclone. How profoundly

God is understood by Lawrence as the fertility in all fecundity,
the author of the seasons in the natural world and the absolute
Lord of life, is expressed in a remarkable passage at the beginning
of his novel *The Rainbow*. This novel incidentally has the most
brilliant descriptions of nature of all his novels; they outdistance
Thomas Hardy in their correlation of human moods and the
moods of nature. Consider the violence and vividness of the
sensual imagery in the following citation:

> Heaven and earth was teeming around them, and how
> should this cease? They felt the rush of sap in spring, they
> knew the wave that cannot halt, but every year throws
> forward the seed to begetting, and, falling back, leaves the
> young-born on the earth. They knew the intercourse
> between heaven and earth, sunshine drawn into the breast
> and bowels, the rain sucked up in the daytime, nakedness
> that comes under the wind in autumn, showing the birds'
> nests no longer worth hiding.

Similarly in a short story, "The Sun," Lawrence develops the idea
that the sun is a lover, and sun worship an act of submission to the
sun's penetration. It was a quite deliberate revival of an element
of the old pagan fertility cults by Lawrence. He believed that the
taming of the flesh in traditional Christianity, combined with that
oscillation between prudishness and prurience which was the
legacy of the late Victorian church, proved that an evisceration
had taken place through excessive spiritualizing of both God and
his creatures. In brief, Lawrence maintained that modern Christians believed in a hygienic and housebroken deity.

   His second criticism of Christianity was that its idea of human
nature was too cerebral and disembodied. In his essay on Poe,
Lawrence excoriates the destructive analytic tendency of the cold
intellect. "To *know* a living thing is to kill it," he writes, and
adds, "for this reason, the desirous consciousness, THE SPIRIT, is
a vampire" and "to try to *know* any living being is to try to suck
the life out of that being." Unquestionably Lawrence feels that

Paul's relationship with Miriam, his first love, in *Sons and Lovers* (1913) is a failure because it attempts to be a love between disembodied spirits. Paul says to Miriam:

> See, you are a nun. I have given you what I would give a holy nun . . . . In all our relations no body enters. I do not talk to you through the senses, rather through the spirit. That is why we cannot love in the common sense. . . . If people marry, they must live together as affectionate humans, not as two souls.

Paul has interpreted Miriam's attitude correctly. In her prayers for Paul she asks to be able to love him "as Christ would, who died for the souls of men." We shall be reminded of this irony of the concentration on *souls*, when in *The Man Who Died* (1928), Lawrence will show the Resurrected Man saying to Madeleine:

> I asked them all to serve me with the corpse of their love. And in the end I offered them only the corpse of my love. This is my body—take and eat my corpse . . . I wanted them to love with dead bodies.

Lawrence pleads for the return to the instinctual life rather than the life of the intellect, for the genuine recognition of the role of the body and the senses in a fully human life, arguing that Christianity wants us to be disembodied angels before we have learned the tenderness of human communication that is possible through the five senses fully employed in love.

The third criticism of Christianity has been partly touched on already. It is the challenging claim that the Christ presented by Christianity is too morbid and too pessimistic a portrait, insufficiently life-affirming. The dominant image of Christ in Christianity, Lawrence argues, is the crucified Christ, a vast, terrifying, and threatening image of pain, anguish, and torture. As early as 1915 Lawrence fulminated against the contemporary Church for its miserable and morbid view of the resurrection story: its emphasis

on the cross, the wounds, the tomb, above and beyond the "pale
face of Resurrection" for this emphasis left "half of the year of
the soul [the Christian calendar] . . . cold and historyless," and it
also meant that the "religious drama of life was ended at thirty-
three." The theme of *The Man Who Died* can be seen thirteen
years earlier in *The Rainbow* (1915), where Christ affirms that the
Resurrection is to life, not to death, and soliloquizes in this way:

> Can I not then walk this earth in gladness being risen from
> sorrow? Can I not eat with my brother happily, and with
> joy kiss my beloved, after my resurrection, celebrate my
> marriage in the flesh with feastings, go about my business
> eagerly, in the joy of my fellows? Is heaven impatient for
> me that I should hurry off, or that I should linger pale and
> untouched? Is the flesh which was crucified become as
> poison to the crowds in the street, or is it as a strong glad-
> ness and hope to them, as the first flower blossoming out
> of the earth's humus?

Lawrence's fourth criticism of Christianity lies in the fact that
he found its conception of life too renunciatory, too lacking in
passion, too tepid. Lawrence believed that life should be a marriage feast celebrated with great joy and dancing, but Christianity
has turned life into a funeral procession with long faces, unnatural
quietness, and a creeping tempo. Especially was this to be seen in
Christianity's conception of love, which was tame and legalistic.
Holy wedlock had become—to use A.P. Herbert's phrase—"holy
deadlock." In the novel *Women in Love*, Birkin expounds to her
lover Gerald Crich on the theme of the terrible constriction and
narrowing of personalities that can take place in conventional
marriages: "It's a sort of hunting in couples: the world all in
couples, each couple in its own little house, watching its own little
interests, and stewing in its own little privacy—it's the most repul-
sive thing on earth." The glory of Lawrence lies in his sacramental
view of love and sex, which will be discussed later, but it is at the
same time clear that to him the customary marriage blessed at the
altars of the Church seems singularly unadventurous and

unromantic, insufficiently earthy. Such a marriage all too easily degenerates into a mere instrument of mutual satisfaction, or else, becomes the arena of a struggle of wills, a struggle that has been cynically defined as the making of two into one and a life-long struggle to determine *which* that one is. Lawrence believed profoundly in the spontaneity, honesty, naturalness, mutuality, fidelity, and full "phallic" sexuality of marriage. Sexual union was, in the strictest sense, the "deed of life"—to use the very apt title of Julian Moynahan's admirable book on Lawrence—and in a secondary sense it fructified human relationships.

In sum, then, Lawrence's case against the Christianity of his day is a series of formidable charges: that its God was moralistic, that its idea of human being was too intellectual and ghostly, that its concept of Christ was too morbid, and that its understanding of human existence was too renunciatory. Life should be celebration, not condemnation, a phoenix of fire, not a decomposing crow!

Having expressed the conventional case against Lawrence, and expounded the case of Lawrence against Christianity, it is now high time to present the case *for* Lawrence, that is, the grateful recognition of those new insights into life's meaning which Lawrence offers in his novels. For he has little interest in narrative or in character-building or in plot; Lawrence is a didactic novelist who uses nature as his background and human beings as his symbols. He writes always with a high seriousness: "I often think one ought to be able to pray before one works—and then leave it to the Lord. . . . I always feel as if I stood naked for the fire of Almighty God to go through me—and it's rather an awful feeling. One has to be so terribly religious to be an artist." Lawrence is unquestionably a preacher in his novels.

His greatest insight is the rediscovery of the centrality of love in life and in religion. Certainly Augustine and before

him Paul had seen this, but late Victorian Christians had accepted
too radical a divergence between heavenly and earthly love,
between *agape* and *eros*. The soul was the recipient of Christ's
love and the responsive ardor of the mystic was cleansed of all
bodily clinging. Lawrence insists in his novels that it is through
the body that we humans love, not apart from the body. He
wants to end all leering about human love, all shame in sexuality,
and so he is more grievously misunderstood if thought to be an
advocate of promiscuity. His great American friend, Earl
Brewster, says of him; "Never during my years of intimacy with
him have I ever known him to tell a vulgar story, nor to joke or
speak lightly of sex. . . ." It was quite in character for him to
write to Lady Ottoline Morrell: "God forbid that I should be
taken as urging loose sex activity. There is a brief time for sex and
a long time when sex is out of place. But when it is out of place as
an activity there should still be a large and quiet space in the consciousness where it lives quiescent." He then adds, rather whims-
ically, "Old people can have a lovely quiescent sort of sex, like
apples, leaving the young free for their sort." Lawrence wanted
gratefully to give the body its due.

But this did not mean physical love is for Lawrence merely a
rutting exercise, the "rub and tickle" of Dylan Thomas's poem,
though it is tactile and not a platonic experience. It should be
remembered that the original title of *Lady Chatterley's Lover* was
"Tenderness." There Lawrence's manifesto is delivered through
the character of Mellors the gamekeeper: "I stand for the touch
of bodily awareness between human beings . . . and the touch of
tenderness." He adds, "Sex is the closest of all touch." One
cannot, I think, come closer than to say of *Lady Chatterley's
Lover* that in this novel Lawrence claims that love is sacramental—
it is the most sacred and holy expression of devoted love, and
expression of the divine creativity itself. One critical study of this
idea in the novel affirms that "the act of love is the communion-
rite of this novel." When contrasted with the clandestine character of sexual love in the Victorian age, and the perversity of sexual
love in the Edwardian age, the attitude of Lawrence seems to me
to be entirely joyous and liberating.

Indeed, I am all the more respectful of it when I think of what he was battling against, for Lawrence criticizes two inadequate conceptions of sexual love in *Lady Chatterley's Lover*. Before his paralysis, Constance Chatterley and her husband had looked on sexual union as casual, as almost obsolescent in a truly intellectual society; that was one way of cheapening sex. Another form of this cheapening is illustrated by Constance's relationship with her dramatist lover, Michaelis, where the expression of sexuality was exclusively sensate, mere mutual titillation. The meeting of Constance with Mellors develops into a relationship that awakes Constance to passion, warmth, and beauty, while Mellors himself returns from lonely isolation to life and warm-hearted love. Love is, indeed, a communion, a religious rite.

Now it can, of course, be argued that this is to place too great a value on human love, until it becomes an idolatry. There are times when Lawrence becomes unintentionally amusing in the glorification of sexuality, especially in his poems. It is solemnly and unintentionally diverting when he writes of the love antics of whales, sporting in the deep:

> Then the great bull lies up against his bride
> in the deep blue of the sea
> as mountain pressing against mountain

But the love-in of the leviathans becomes ludicrous when we go on to read:

> And over the bridge of the whale's strong
>   phallus, linking the wonder of whales
> the burning archangels under the sea keep
>   passing, back and forth.

I won't embarrass the fleshy shade of Lawrence by asking him what those two lines mean! On this point it is important only to insist on Lawrence's recovery in his novels on a rich, full, tender, joyous appreciation of human sexual love.

His splendid second rediscovery was a profound sense of the interdependence of men and women, and their dependence upon the world of animals and flowers. Lawrence was a nature poet and a great walker in the country whose sixth sense—the sense of wonder—was always alert. He looked at the created world in wonder and awe, sensitive even to the changing temperature and direction of the currents of air. The tactile sense was very strongly developed in Lawrence; it is no surprise that he was a painter, but only that he never became a sculptor. His five senses were marvellously sensitive antennae for recording sensations. If this sense of the unity of man and nature were consistently expressed it could be called pantheism, the identification of God with all created things. Often, however, Lawrence veers from pantheism to dualism, a view that sees the world primarily in terms of a conflict between powers of good and evil, and even to a dualistic view of darkness and light where the two powers are complementary, not antithetical. This view clearly predominates in *The Plumed Serpent* (1926), where Kate, the protagonist, involves herself with two men who respectively stand for passion and for reflection, for the instinctive and the rational life. They become, in a sense, incarnations of the sun god and the moon god, the day and the night, the light and the dark, the two primal spirits. Kate comes to see that both of them are necessary to her.

Lawrence rarely depicts the two powers equally, as he has done in this novel. Usually his depiction strongly emphasizes the dark and sensual gods, the chthonic powers, for he believed that the God of light, the cerebral and spiritual, had been too much the human preoccupation during the Christian era, and saw it as his mission to proclaim the authority of the dark gods and so restore the balance to life. It is in *The Man Who Died* that Lawrence achieves the perfect balance, joining the spirituality of Jesus to the dark fertility of the ancient pagan rite of Isis and Osiris. Linked to this appreciation of the deep bond between human beings and the natural world, moreover, is Lawrence's strong and vehement protest against the industrial befoulment and the pollution of nature. His own native Eastwood, a colliery district on the edge of both Sherwood Forest and the peak district of Derbyshire, was a symbol of the new ugliness, where men were blackened with the coal, their lungs weakened by silicosis, and beaten into sullenness by their profiteering and domineering employers. *Sons and Lovers* (1913) etches Lawrence's native setting to the life, a symbol of a stunted society which Lawrence wishes to return to nature and naturalness as avidly as Rousseau.

If religion is to be defined as a sense of the overarching wonder of life, or as Rudolf Otto has suggested in *The Idea of the Holy*, as a sense of awe that both fascinates and frightens (*mysterium tremendum et fascinans*), then unquestionably Lawrence was a deeply religious man. If on the other hand the Christian doctrine of creation stresses that God is transcendent over and independent of his world, Lawrence is only partly Christian; while he celebrates the goodness of the world, and while he recognizes the role of love and fecundity in all creation, Lawrence does not acknowledge the transcendence of God. But the recognition of wonder as the appropriate response to the majesty and mystery in the universe is fully and appropriately Christian and cosmic. So Lawrence's third value is to recognize that in a universe for which there is a scientific explanation, the mythic, poetic, imaginative mode is appropriate for the expression of religious values. Such values are divined in myth and symbol, rather than dissected and explained in discursive thought. As Lawrence said, "You can only analyze *dead* protoplasm." The imagination is the language of vitality in action. Lawrence recognized that traditional Christianity had cast a halo over ordinary life by relating the Christian calendar to the rhythms and recurrences of the calendar of nature. "So the children," he writes in *The Rainbow*, "lived the year of Christianity, the epic of the soul of mankind. Year by year, the inner, unknown drama went on in them, their hearts were born and came to fulness, suffered on the cross, gave up the ghost, and rose again to unnumbered days, untired, having at least this rhythm of eternity in a ragged inconsequential life."

Lawrence knew that religion lives most completely in the imagination. He recognized how completely his childhood faith was still operative in him, chiefly through the familiar hymns he sang as a boy. These hymns, he asserts, "live and glisten in the depths of the man's consciousness in undimmed wonder, because they have not been subjected to any criticism or analysis." He was, Lawrence declared, eternally grateful for the wonder with which religious teaching filled his childhood, and presumably for the assurance it brought to sing

> Sun of my soul, thou Saviour dear,
> It is not night if Thou be near.

C.S. Lewis has affirmed that it is only when the adolescent imagination is kept alive by feeding it heroic legends, myths, and sagas is it possible to prepare the spirit to receive Christian truth in a technocratic, liberal, and automated age. God's dealings with his people must be marvelous, mysterious, magical; to this sublime truth Lawrence bears witness. In another way Lawrence showed himself to be a religious man: in his desire to create a community of the spirit which would live in contradiction of the money-grabbing materialism and militarism of the century. He desired to found a colony of like-minded friends away from "this world of war and squalor. . . where there shall be no money but a sort of communism as far as the necessaries of life go and some real decency." It is odd to think of Lawrence as a modern pilgrim father gratefully leaving Europe behind him, but not too odd when one recalls that Lawrence's upbringing was that of a Congregationalist. There are strong social implications of the risen life of Christ in the flesh in a companion essay (entitled *The Risen Lord*) he wrote to *The Man Who Died*, which presents Christ battling for the sake of the crowd with the foes of Mammon, false pride, and vulgar materialism. Religion was a radical rebellion against the anaesthesia of the social conscience which had set in among the conventional bourgeoisie.

What, then, was Lawrence? A Christian, a pagan hostile to Christianity, or a Christian heretic? While, as Father Martin Jarrett-Kerr of the Anglican Communion of the Resurrection writes, Lawrence "can teach the Christians lessons they should have known but forgotten," this is not enough to make a Christian prophet of him. Jarrett-Kerr properly sees fit to praise Lawrence for his recognition of "the ISness rather than the OUGHTness of religion." It is clear that Lawrence takes very seriously what is given here and now by God and that he affirms that the body is the central focus of man's interconnectedness with men, and he sees that the resurrection of Christ is the resurrection of the flesh—all significant and insufficiently stressed points of Christian truth. Where, then, is Lawrence's understanding of Christianity deficient?

He had a sense of God as a cosmic power and a creator, but not as both transcendent and personal. He also had a sense of the holy which might be said to approximate the Holy Spirit. What Lawrence entirely lacked was a sense of God as the *Father* Almighty and a sense of Jesus Christ as the eternal Son of God, and of the Holy Spirit as the bond of love between them. We may describe him as T.S. Eliot did, as one who "lived all his life on the spiritual level" or more generously and gratefully, we may acknowledge Lawrence as prophet of the power of love, divine and human, but a prophet incognito, or as an original would-be reviser and reformer of Christianity, which is what Christian heretics have usually been. But to adjective and noun an equal emphasis must be given, for 'Christian' and 'heretic' are interdependent terms, and I suspect they are widely applicable.

CHARLES WILLIAMS

Supernatural Thrillers

Who was Charles Williams? The answer is, an obscure editor in the London office of the Oxford University Press, who was prevented by the reduced circumstances of his family from continuing his education beyond the second year of London University, and who was afterwards appointed Lecturer in English at Oxford University. The same accomplished and largely self-educated man died in the city of Oxford at the age of fifty-nine, after having written over forty books, including several hundred poems, plays, and reviews, one short story, and seven 'eschatological' novels, dealing with death, judgment, heaven, hell and purgatory—the traditional orthodox 'last things' in Christian theology. In fact, the novel that provides the focus of our particular study, *All Hallows Eve*, begins during the minute after death. Such a topic requires a vivid and sustained imagination, and imagination Williams had in abundance.

Two critical comments only are needed to indicate the variety of reactions to Williams's work, comments that run the gamut from rhapsodical enthusiasm to utter bewilderment at the obscurity and or even relevance of his themes. The critic F.R. Leavis excoriates his "preoccupation with the 'horror of evil' as evidence of an arrest at the schoolboy (and -girl) stage rather than of spiritual maturity." In contrast, his friend C.S. Lewis has said of the later poems, "They seem to me, both for the soaring and gorgeous novelty of their technique and for their very profound wisdom to be among the two or three most valuable books of verse produced in this century."

This very controversial novelist, poet, critic, and lay theologian belonged to the famous Oxford circle of "Inklings" who met regularly at the Eagle and Child Inn on St. Giles' for learned and frank discussions. These friends included some of the most

creative religious minds in England. Among them were J.R.
Tolkien, author of the trilogy *Lord of the Rings*, which was first
read aloud to this group, and C.S. Lewis, one of the best contemporary apologists for Christianity in his broadcasts for the B.B.C.
and a writer of novels and science fiction of such quality as
Perelandra. Dorothy L. Sayers was an associate, although not a
member of the group, a writer of detective stories and author of
the most distinguished of all modern cycles of radio plays, *Born to
be King,* a life of Christ, which the B.B.C. broadcasts each year in
Passion Week. Other members of the inner circle included Owen
Barfield, lawyer and man of letters, who later taught English at
Drew University, and the distinguished Dominican scholar Father
Gervase Mathew.

Born in St. Albans in 1886, a cathedral center and the traditional site of the first martyr to Christianity in England, Williams
was brought up a High Church Anglican and acquired a classical
education at St. Albans Grammar School. After an all too brief
two years at London University, he found a post at Amen House,
near St. Paul's Cathedral in London at the offices of the Oxford
University Press. While in London he lectured on religion and
literature to groups of working men in adult education institutes,
men whom Williams called a "center of power," a new source of
energy for the culture, in a lecture he presented at a conference of
academics and clergy. He lived a quiet life, was happily married in
1917 at the age of thirty to Florence Conway, who bore him a son
named Michael. At the outbreak of war Williams was declared
unfit for military service and he moved to Oxford. He died shortly after VE day and was sorely missed.

W.H. Auden said, in a tribute to Williams, "In his company
one felt twice as intelligent and infinitely nicer than, out of it, one
knew one's self to be." C.S. Lewis averred that in the absence of
Williams his friends felt that "some principle of liveliness and
cohesion had been withdrawn from the whole party: lacking him,
we did not completely possess one another."

It is only the obscurity of some of his writing, and the unfamiliarity with some of the theological concepts such as "substituted love" and "co-inherence," that have prevented his books from reaching a wider circle. His novels are thoughtful, imaginatively presented, and have an uncompromising fidelity to orthodox Christianity. My procedure will be to mention each of the novels briefly, then to discuss the major theological concepts of Williams, and finally to analyze the two mature novels in detail, namely, *Descent into Hell* and *All Hallows' Eve*.

His first novel, *War in Heaven*, appeared in 1930. It is the story of Gregory Persimmons's attempt to secure the Holy Grail (the chalice used by Christ at the Last Supper) in order to be able to unite himself with the supreme source of power. His aim is to dominate the entire world and even to be victor over death, but his attempt is foiled by the faith and courage of an Anglican archdeacon and his friends.

The contrast of the attitudes of grab and grace is depicted with equal vividness in the next novel, *Many Dimensions*, published in 1931. Many seekers after power, especially Sir Giles, wish to possess a magical stone from Solomon's crown. With this in their hold they will be able to destroy their enemies, while other characters desire the magical stone to fulfill other ambitions, all equally at variance with the common good.

A third novel, *The Place of the Lion*, appeared the same year. This fantasy describes the confusion and fear that erupt in the world through the release of archetypal beasts, and again the confrontation exhibits the difference of good and evil persons.

The fourth novel, *The Greater Trumps*, came out in 1932. Another magical object, the original Tarot pact of cards, evokes the desire in two men, Aaron and Henry, to unite themselves with the power creating and controlling the matter of life. They are, however, resisted by other characters who oppose the perversion

of such power to private, egotistical ends. The important theme
of substitution and exchange, which Williams will fully develop in
the two final novels, appears in rather shadowy and vague form in
this narrative. *Shadows of Ecstasy* (1933) also turns on the theme
of the abuse of power. The novel tells of a political revolution in
Africa led by a man who wants to take control of Europe and who
claims to have power over death itself.

The two most mature novels appeared after longer intervals,
thus providing the author with greater opportunity to develop his
major theological themes. The sixth novel, *Descent into Hell*, was
published in 1937. Its theme is the contrast between the utter
isolation and ultimate nonexistence of the introverted self, and the
openness of the other-regarding self living by the sacrifices of substitution and exchange.

The final novel, *All Hallows' Eve*, appeared in 1945, the year
of Williams's death. It is a profound exposition of the author's
understanding of the theology of romantic love. The central evil
character is Simon the Clerk, a sinister triple personality who is
a vile shadow image of the Holy Trinity. He uses sorcery to gain
dominance over the whole world through spirits at his command.
His opponents employ the loving art of exchange and substitution
and ultimately defeat his Satanism.

Williams clearly intends his novels to indicate the vast difference between those who interpret Nature as ultimate and autono-
mous, and others who claim that Nature is subject to supernatural
forces beyond time, space, and human thought. However,
Williams sees the two realms as existing parallel to each other. He
recognizes that in Christian tradition there have been two different
approaches to the knowledge and experience of God. These are
known as the negative and affirmative ways. In the negative way
God is reached by detaching the soul from all entities that are less
than God, and this method rejects all images. For Christians,
however, God is not only other than and beyond our capacity to
understand, that is, transcendent. He is also immanent, dwelling

within us, and in the world. Hence everything in the world which God has created is also an image of him—however inadequate and imperfect an image of his perfection. The way of affirmation acknowledges this, and accepts all things in love, not for their own sake, but as images of the divine.

As Dante in gazing on Beatrice glimpsed the perfection of God, so the first wonder and awe of human love is a striking experience of the affirmative way. Williams believed, moreover, that the lover and the poet know the way of affirmation best, even if the greatest mystics, like St. Teresa of Avila and St. John of the Cross, chose the negative way of reaching union with God.

So the beginning of the soul's choice of the way is what Williams termed the 'romantic experience.' This is a special moment of intense vision in which some image of the created universe is seen as expressing and embodying the transcendent Good. There is, however, as Williams acknowledged, a great danger in this approach—that the image of the beloved may be treated less as a person than as a mere instrument of sensual gratification.

One example of the appropriate response to this vision is found in the novel *Shadows of Ecstasy*. Williams's own views are expressed by Sir Bernard Travers, who is considering his son's infatuation for a girl named Rosamund. He knows the girl is of average mind and character, but admits that in his boy's eyes she appears divine, nor does he dismiss his son as a blind idiot for that reason. He concludes that

> a thing that seemed had at least the truth of its seeming.
> Sir Bernard's mind refused to allow it more but also refused
> to allow it less. It was for each man to determine what the
> truth of each seeming was . . . . A thing might not be true
> because it appeared so to him, but it was no less likely to
> be true because everyone denied it. The eyes of Rosamund
> might or might not hold the secret origin of day or night,

but if they apparently did then they apparently did, and
it would be silly to deny it and equally silly not to relish it.

It is clear that Williams is willing to allow that the beauty
apparently in the eye of the beholder may in fact have divine
origins, although the life of faith requires us to distinguish
between necessary, essential faith and indiscriminate credulity.

The inappropriate response to the first moment of vision is
illustrated in *Descent into Hell.* One of the characters, Lawrence
Wentworth, a historian, is frustrated in his longing for a woman
who does not return his affection. He consequently chooses a
succubus in her exact image, which is totally subservient to his
will, unlike the woman it copies. Closing himself in his house and
relinquishing all interest in the real world outside, Wentworth is
totally absorbed by this self-loving activity. Finally, he even
refuses to recognize the presence of the real woman, when in a
moment of terror she turns to him for help.

A central concept in Williams's interpretation is the idea of
'substitution' or 'exchange.' In his view exchange is an essential
component of individual, familial, social, and political life. In
addition, Williams intends this term 'exchange' both literally and
practically. All close personal relationships demand sacrifice, the
free gift to others of a part of one's personality—whether it be the
relationship of lovers, parents to children, teachers to pupils, and
that division of labor and of gifts that is expressed in the body
politic. But those who give over parts of their personality also
receive from others. Williams asserts that the taunt of scoffers
made to Christ on the cross was profoundly true: "Others He
saved; Himself He cannot save." Thus since we are unable to save
ourselves, others must be allowed to save us while we are involved
in the saving of still others. In fact, however, it is Christ in them
and in us who is the ultimate Savior. As we shall see, this doctrine
is admirably exemplified in the last two novels.

The conception of 'substitution' may seem less impracticable
if a common experience is used as an analogy. Mary McDermott

Shideler provides such an analogy—that of firemen taking the burden of risks for others, "safeguarding the forest or the city by placing themselves in jeopardy, substituting their skills, equipment and lives for the inadequacies of other citizens."

It is the cross of Christ itself which is the greatest paradigm and act of substitution and exchange. Williams writes movingly of the supreme act of redemption:

In the last reaches of that living death to which we are exposed He substituted himself for us. He submitted in our stead to the full results of the Law which is He. We may believe He was generous if we know that He was just. By that central substitution, which was the thing added to the Incarnation, He became everywhere the centre of, and everywhere He energized and reaffirmed, all our substitutions and exchanges. He took what remained after the Fall of the torn web of humanity in all times and places, and not so much by a miracle of healing as by a growth within that made it whole.

A complementary doctrine that Williams elaborates in the two final novels is that of 'coinherence.' He affirms with full theological orthodoxy that the God of Christians is a dynamic unity of three persons, the Holy Trinity. It is the supreme relationship of mutual Love. Since human beings are made in the divine image, this pattern of coinherence is partially realized in social relationships on earth. Every expression of a just political order is an image of the divine order in Heaven. Williams's term of the larger political unity, mirroring the mutual gifts of the citizens, is the City. As every earthly city exists through the sharing of different kinds of labor, distinguished or drab, and these are, whether recognized or not, substitutions or exchanges, so every city is a shadow of the Heavenly City.

Descent into Hell, considered by some to be the best novel
Williams wrote, provides an admirable analysis of two ways of
interpreting reality, the materialist and the theological. Its background is a well-to-do London suburb, called Battle Hill. A group
living in this community proposes to produce a new play written
by the most famous poet of the day, Peter Stanhope, who resides
on the Hill and has promised to assist the actors in the production
of the play. Pauline Anstruther, a young woman in the cast of the
play, has lived for some time in a state of continual anxiety and
thus catches the attention of the playwright. She explains to Stanhope that off and on for years she has seen a double of herself, not
someone exactly like her and not a hallucination, and that she is
convinced that when she meets this other self face to face she will
die. Meantime, her grandmother, Margaret Anstruther, is slowly
dying with great serenity of mind. Also in the novel is a nameless
man who had committed suicide a year earlier and who now
wanders about the hill, and he is seen first by old Margaret and
then by her granddaughter Pauline. Another famous inhabitant of
the Hill, also a celebrity, is the historian Lawrence Wentworth,
who pursues his independent search for happiness that ends in the
'descent into hell' which gives the novel its title.

Wentworth's way of reaching hell is simplicity itself. When he
is jilted by Adela, the woman he desires, in favor of a younger
suitor, Wentworth rejects the inconvenient fact from his mind
and consoles himself with a wholly imaginary mistress with
Adela's form and voice, but a mistress who is utterly pliant. When
another historian is given an award that he had hoped for, Wentworth persuades himself that the award is merely a political favor.
Embittered with resentment at these other persons, he withdraws
to such a degree from his neighbors and colleagues that finally
Wentworth neglects to draw attention to a minor error in the
costuming of the play when called upon for an expert's opinion,
even though it will involve no effort from him and little from
anyone else. Thus he withdraws from friends and fellow scholars,
from all the acts of giving and receiving by which biological and
social life are maintained. Outwardly Wentworth is still a living

man, but inwardly he lives in a timeless solitude without memory, and with only a sense of the interminable boredom and monotony of negation.

Wholly contrasted with this way to hell is the way that leads to heaven. The latter way is embodied in Stanhope the poet and Margaret Anstruther, the dying woman, who introduce Pauline to the way of exchange, or—in the phrase of Williams—of "substituted love," the way of giving and receiving that transcend mere human nature. Stanhope, having learned of Pauline's fear of meeting the *doppelganger*, an image or double of herself, offers to carry her fear for her, just as if a burden of fear could be transferred like a jar of honey from one person to another. Stanhope tells Pauline: "It's a fact of experience. If you give a weight to me, you can't be carrying it yourself; all I'm asking you to do is to notice that blazing truth." Not only is this the practical thing to do, he continues, but the nature of the universe demands it. As he says,

> If you want to live in pride and division and anger, you can. But if you will be part of the best of us, and live and laugh and be ashamed with us, then you must . . . give your burden up to someone else, and you must carry someone else's burden. I haven't made the universe and it isn't my fault. But I'm sure that this is a law of the universe. . . .

Pauline, with great reluctance and disbelief at first, allows Stanhope to carry her fear and endure in her stead the panic she had anticipated.

After Pauline has been initiated into the acts of substituted love, through Stanhope's transference of her burden of fear to himself, Pauline in her turn is offered the opportunity to bear the burden of another. The appeal for her help comes from one of her own ancestors, who had been martyred four centuries earlier and stands in some relationship to the spirit of the suicide

wandering on the Hill. It is possible for Pauline to answer this
request because she is living in the present, and the time in which
he had lived had been the present for him. In the infinite contemporaneity which is eternity, all present moments coinhere, so
Pauline is able to meet her ancestor and carry his fear, and it is in
this act that her meeting with herself eventually takes place.

The source of all acts of substituted love is, as we have seen,
the cross of Christ, and all sacrifice is based solidly upon it. The
free offering of one's self to take over the sufferings of another,
which is substituted love, is the central theme of the novel we are
about to consider, *All Hallows Eve*. A second central theme of
this novel is the coinherence or simultaneous existence of what we
erroneously call the "natural" and the "supernatural." Another
idea the novel sets forth is the essential holiness of all things, with
the single exception of some attitudes of the will from which
corruption or abuse spreads. A fourth idea is Williams's development of the understanding of Purgatory as a process of the purifi-
cation of the soul after death, on its way to the abode of the
blessed.

The heroine of *All Hallows Eve* is Lester Furnival, a young
woman of twenty-five who has only been married some six
months. At the opening of the novel she is dead, standing on
Westminster Bridge, a few steps away from the place on the
Thames embankment where she has just been killed by the accidental crash of a fighter plane. It is 1945 and the fighting in
Europe has ended. Around her the city of London is familiar
and yet at the same time vacuous and ghostly. She sees her
husband, Richard, approaching and she makes a spontaneous
gesture of warding him off as he reaches out to her, and then he
seems to disappear. At that instant she realizes that it is not the
city that is a ghost, but she herself.

She then meets another girl, Evelyn, a life-long close acquain-

tance but not a friend, who has also been killed. Evelyn is a
constant complainer and groaner, who tags along with Lester.

About a month afterwards, Lester's widower husband Richard
Furnival visits his friend, Jonathan Drayton, a painter. There he
sees a portrait of a man Drayton has painted known as Simon the
Clerk, the leader of a highly popular cult. The mother of Jonathan's fiancée, Betty Wallingford, known as Lady Wallingford, is
Simon the Clerk's chief supporter and helper. The portrait,
which infuriates Lady Wallingford and which she has rejected,
depicts the Clerk with an expression of imbecilic emptiness and
his followers are shown as flowing into a cleft of a rock like so
many small images of their master, who resembles a huge beetle.
Jonathan has also painted another picture, a view of the center of
London irradiated by the light of the dawn. Throughout the story
this picture changes slightly, with the quality of the light becoming ever more glorious and more mysterious, symbolizing the
brilliance of the Eternal City shining through London.

When Simon the Clerk sees his portrait he likes it, but he also
dislikes the painting of the City of London. Simon is a magician,
learned in the secrets of the Cabbala, a mystical occultism of
medieval rabbinical development. His title, "clerk," signifies
"cleric" or "clergyman," and he is a kind of demonic priest whose
followers call "the Father." Although his face is ageless Simon
is over two hundred years old and he has created two simulacra,
or images of himself. One image is winning millions of disciples
in Russia, and the other is gaining millions in China. The "big
three" are planning to meet and this meeting will suit Simon
admirably, because it will be the occasion of his taking over the
world.

He is also the father of Betty Wallingford, who was conceived
not in love, but with cold calculation for a diabolical purpose. She
is to be murdered demonically, so that she will be wholly Simon's
accomplice and servant. Simon, like Simon Magus before him, is a
corrupt Faustus and a type of the anti-Christ. Prolonging his own
life magically, he has

refused the possibilities of death. He would not go to it, as that other child of a Jewish girl had done. That other had refused safeguard and miracle; he had refused the achievement of security. He had gone into death—as the rest of mankind go—ignorant and in pain. The clerk had set himself to decline pain and ignorance. So that now he had not any capacities but those he could himself gain.

Simon the Clerk has embraced the very temptations that Christ rejected in the wilderness.

The whole dramatic interest of the novel concerns itself with the efforts made on both natural and supernatural levels to save Betty from the clutches of the Clerk. Jonathan Drayton is the chief actor on the natural level and Lester Furnival on the supernatural; but as the supernatural is more significant than the natural, so Lester's efforts are more significant than Jonathan's.

At a deeper level the interest centers on Lester's adjustment to her new existence, and her gradual movement from the Lesser City to the Greater City. The mode and means of her growth and advancement is her instinctive, disinterested desire to come to Betty's rescue when, by chance and on impulse, Lester finds herself standing by at a moment that is crucial in the Clerk's designs on Betty. Later she extends the willingness to give, and even to suffer, on behalf of the unresponsive and utterly selfish Evelyn— thus her love for the loveless mirrors Christ's.

As Betty is recalled from the brink of death by Lester's intercession, the living girl herself begins her spiritual progress, growing and maturing in radiant joy.

Another factor in Betty's salvation has been the "wise water" —the holy water, consecrated solely by the intention with which a loving nurse, in secret defiance of Lady Wallingford, had baptized her as a child. At the end she is willing to substitute herself even unto death if this is necessary, and thus acquires the holy

power to heal once more the souls whom the Clerk had falsely
healed by magic and who, on the Clerk's downfall, have fallen
back into their sufferings. Just as the stories of Lester's and
Betty's spiritual growth show the possibilities for goodness, so
does the deterioration of Evelyn show the possibilities of evil.
She resists any call to more generous living, and clings to petty,
malicious, possessive pleasures. Perhaps the most devastating
comment on Evelyn is Betty's relief and even gladness that
Evelyn is dead, because her death has liberated Betty from her
perpetually melancholy disposition.

The theme of coinherence, of the simultaneity of all periods
of time, is absolutely central to the novel. Lester has glimpses of
superimposed layers and layers of the city of London, from the
days when it was only a large village in open country to its modern
dense population. These different periods all occur simultaneous-
ly and coinhere in London. In turn, London coinheres with all
other earthly cities and with the City of God, of which all earthly
cities are but dim images, as man is a dim image of God. This is
how Williams puts it:

> There around her lay not only London, but all cities—
> coincident yet each distinct; or else, in another mode,
> lying by each other as the districts of one city lie. She
> could, had the time and her occasions permitted, have
> gone to any she chose—any time and place that men had
> occupied or would occupy. There was no huge metropo-
> lis in which she would have been lost in all that contemp-
> oraneous mass. . . . Here citizenship meant relationship
> and knew it; its citizens lived new acts or lived the old at
> will. What on earth is only in the happiest moments of
> friendship or love was now normal. Lester's new friend-
> ship with Betty was but the merest flicker, but it was
> the flicker which now carried her soul.

The theme of substituted love is only hinted at here, in the
phrase, "for here citizenship meant relationship and knew it."

The acme and apex of substituted love is, of course, the incarnation and passion of Christ. The truest imitation of him is to carry out the substitution by the free unreserved gift of oneself to carry the trial, burden, pain, temptation or penalty of another. That was, as may be recalled, the central theme of the novel preceding this one, *Descent into Hell*, and it is not limited by space or time, either backward or forward.

Williams's "City" is, of course, the City of God as it appears in the Book of Revelation. "And I John saw the holy city . . . descending out of heaven from God, having the glory of God." This City is also the source of St. Augustine's great defense of Christianity, *The City of God*. It is the New Jerusalem. In *All Hallows Eve* there is a special localized sense of the City as applied to secular London and the heart of the city including St. Paul's Cathedral and the Bank of England equally, the latter known as "the Old Lady of Threadneedle Street."

In *All Hallows Eve*, we should note, the capacity to make acts of substitution is only slowly developed. Lester's progress is achieved through unremitting effort and penitential concern. At first she wishes to cling to the past—her first thought is to wish that her husband would join her, be with her as a prisoner, even if his presence means that he must also die. This possessiveness, entangled with the passion of love and sometimes confused with it, is an echo of Milton's *Paradise Lost*. In that poem, to which Williams wrote a famous introduction and interpretation, Eve first thinks after eating the forbidden fruit, she will invite Adam to share it and be equal with her, and then thinks she would prefer to have control over him, and finally has a more selfish thought:

> . . . but what if God have seen,
> And death ensue? Then I shall be no more;
> And Adam, wedded to another Eve,
> Shall live with her enjoying, I extinct!
> A death to think! Confirmed, then, I resolve
> Adam shall share with me in bliss or woe.

It is fear that dominates Lester at that early stage of her pilgrimage.

When Lester realizes that Betty is crying in the magician's house, her first impulse is to do nothing, even to rationalize the situation and say that it will be better for Betty to learn to stand on her own two feet. At that moment Evelyn, who is standing by, calls out petulantly, "Come away!" At those words, Lester, says the novelist, sees for the first time in her life "a temptation precisely as it is when it has ceased to tempt—repugnant, implausible, mean." She enters the house and that decides her maturity and growth. As she has only recently died, the earth is dearer to Lester than heaven can be. Lonely Richard her husband desires to affirm his love for Lester, and felt a primitive sense of remorse as he thought of some of the errors and shortcomings of their marriage. He felt remorse, "for he was not yet spiritually old enough to repent."

Some critics have felt that there is too much occultism and deviltry in the novel, and that the character Simon is too evil to be convincing. This I do not find a wholly appropriate criticism; the character of Simon is shown to have some admirable qualities, notably, courage, concentration on purpose, immense learning and self-discipline, and the performance of works of healing, however perverted the ends to which these qualities are dedicated. There are also critics who find Lady Wallingford an incredibly wooden creation. She is as bad a mother as Lady Macbeth, who also was prepared to dash out her child's brains, yet Lady Wallingford has also done these deeds out of an unbalanced love for the man to whom she is dedicated. Williams might be expected to have no mercy for her at all, but in her case he shows how patient the divine grace is. In the climactic rites of the demonic Clerk, she commits an accidental substitution, if not a substitution of love. There are possibilities even for her:

> Since in that gift she had desired the good of another and
> not her own, since she had indeed willed to give herself,

the City secluded her passion and took her gift to its own
divine self. She had, almost in a literal physical sense, to
be born again. . . . She was now almost in that state to
which her masters had willed to reduce their child; the
substitution was one of the Acts of the City.

Charles Williams, as I mentioned at the beginning, has been
accused of never having gotten over the immaturity of an obsession with sin and evil, according to F.R. Leavis. It would perhaps
be more to the point to recall that besides the shuddering images
of evil, he has also given us reminders of the Christian promises of
hope, and of the patience, compassion, and power of the holy and
loving purpose of God in Christ. Not the least of Williams's
powers is the reminder that the Christian believes in the communion of saints, the saints of our own time and of all times. The
story begins with *All Hallows Eve*, with Halloween, and its reminder of the evil spirits let loose with the good. The climax of the
story is when Simon the Clerk meets his self-induced end, but the
story closes in the light and holy felicity of All Saints'. Here is a
vision which does greater justice than most to our divine as well as
our demonic possibilities, and to the Christian tradition which
made our Western heritage and may yet renew it.

C.S. LEWIS

The Twofold Conversion

Chad Walsh has called Clive Staples Lewis "the Apostle to Skeptics." C.S. Lewis is a man of both bright intelligence and vivid imagination, who found the exercise of both reason and imagination first obstacles and then avenues to God in a post-Christian world, and who found himself torn by an interior civil war because the two were at variance with one another. This essay explores both the role of the intelligence and the role of the imagination in the protracted and complex conversion of Lewis to Christianity, with the help of his two autobiographies.

The first autobiography appeared in 1933 with the title of *Pilgrim's Regress*. It is a study of the skeptical intellect's arguments against the acceptance of Christianity, and its title recalls John Bunyan's *Pilgrim's Progress*, his classical account of his progress from disbelief to Christianity. Lewis's journey is the reverse of Bunyan's, for he moves from the Christianity of his childhood into the rationalism of unbelief, and into accepting the secular, humanistic myth. *Surprised by Joy: The Shape of My Early Life* is the autobiography which shows how the exercise of the imagination led Lewis to an acceptance of Christianity as his deepest longing and the desire of his spirit. It appeared in 1955 and the title has a double meaning, for its points not only to the joy in all happiness that leads to the supreme joy in God, but also to its private meaning in Lewis's life. Joy Davidman, an American and a great admirer of his writings, eventually married Lewis first in a registry office, so that she could keep her two sons in an English school without repatriation, and shortly afterwards in an Anglican church. Though she had cancer of the bone, there was still a remission for two years before her death—a period of intense and unparalleled joy for this former divorcée and this former bachelor that is referred to in Lewis's later book, *A Grief Observed*.

The range of Lewis's writings deserves consideration and helps
to account for his growing number of readers twenty years after
his death. It is a very significant fact that although C.S. Lewis
died in 1963, he is more widely read now, especially in the United
States, than during his lifetime. Moreover, his serious readers are
found within the ranks of the so-called "New Christians" among
college students as well as among the middle-aged and the venerable readers. Which of his books will live on? This is a natural
question that suggests itself.

Among his theological writings, which are all of a high level,
and all of which strike the unitive, ecumenical note, the one with
the most imaginative verve is certainly the famous *Screwtape
Letters* (1942). The character Screwtape is a minor member of
the 'lowerarchy' run by his Infernal Lowness, Satan, and the book
brilliantly reenacts the way the Evil Spirit captures both clever
and complacent humans. It is also full of wit. Satan is termed
"Our Father Below" and the main speech at the Annual Tempters
Training College describes Screwtape rising to reply to the toast
of the health of the guests: "Mr. Principal, Your Imminence, your
Disgraces, my Thorns, Shades, and Gentledevils . . ." This book
will live on because Lewis has delineated the five stages through
which Satan's strategy moves: first, surround the victim with
worldly friends; second, attack him through his anti-Romanticism
so that he sees the seamy underside of local church and local
Christians; third, attack him through his sexuality; fourth, make
the evil of the world vivid through war; and fifth, put him in the
disappointing trough of middle age.

Lewis's *Seven Chronicles of Narnia* will also last, as triumphs
of the imagination that will continue to charm and edify as long as
Alice in Wonderland will, and provide food for the minds of children and adults.

Critically, as an expert in English literature, two of his books
in that genre will also prove to be long-lived. There is first of all
Lewis's marvelous study of medieval literature, *The Allegory of*

Love (1936), and his excellent volume in the magisterial series, *The Oxford History of the English Literature*, its title being *English Literature in the Sixteenth Century* (1954). An excerpt on the impact of the theology of John Calvin on the religious life gives the flavor:

> The moral severity of [Calvin's] rule laid the foundations of the meaning which the word 'puritan' has since acquired. But this severity did not mean that his theology was, in the last resort, more ascetic than that of Rome. It sprang from his refusal to allow the Roman distinction between the life of 'religion' and the life of the world, between the Counsels and the Commandments. Calvin's picture of the fully Christian life was less hostile to pleasure and to the body than [St. John] Fisher's; but then Calvin demanded that every man should be made to live the fully Christian life. In academic jargon, he lowered the honours standard and abolished the pass degree.

How just and fair Lewis is, and yet how typical that illuminating and witty conclusion to the entire paragraph! The writing of this book took up most of his spare time for eight years, and he referred to the series by its initials of OHEL as the "Oh, Hell! Book." Lewis had the gift of extemporaneous wit. One day this don of Magdalen College, Oxford was eating at the High Table. He was seated next to a Portuguese scholar who boasted that he was a Christopher Columbus of cuisine, to which Lewis somewhat acidly replied: "Rather a vascular de Gama, considering the contents of a sheep's stomach."

How did this gifted man become a Christian, both intellectually and emotionally? At the outset we must consider the vivid, dramatic, and unsparing account of his conversion as he gives it in *Surprised by Joy*. It is a surprising conversion because it was so

reluctant, and this reluctance of Lewis's to accept Christianity
requires some explanation. His conversion took place in two
distinct stages, the first of which was an intellectual conversion to
a belief in God, that is, to theism. At this stage he attempted to
bring his acts, desires, and thoughts into line with what he called
the "Universal Spirit," but Lewis discovered it is almost impossible
for an unbeliever to do the will of God without divine revelation,
as given in the Scriptures, and without recognizing the need of
divine help or grace. He still hoped to be independent of God's
claims and to retain all of his freedom and total liberty—when
God closed in on him. Lewis writes in *Surprised by Joy*:

> In the Trinity Term of 1929, I gave in, and admitted that
> God was God, and knelt and prayed; perhaps, that night,
> the most dejected and reluctant convert in all England. I
> did not then see what is now the most shining and obvious
> thing; the Divine humility which will accept a convert even
> on such terms. The Prodigal son at least walked home on
> his own feet. But who can duly adore that Love which
> will open the high gates to a prodigal who is brought in,
> kicking, struggling, resentful, and darting his eyes in every
> direction for a chance to escape? . . . The hardness of God
> is kinder than the softness of men and His compulsion is
> our liberation.

It must be clearly understood that Lewis's was at first an intellectual conversion to theism, to belief in one God, the ruler of the
universe, and it was a reluctant one, because it infringed on
Lewis's freedom. We see this through the eyes of his pilgrim,
named John, who is Lewis's *alter ego*. In *Pilgrim's Regress* Lewis
clearly objected to the fact that obedience to God would restrict
the ethical options open to him. When his pilgrim character John
is at the end of his tether at the bottom of the Canyon, he gazes
up at the cliffs and the narrow sky between and he considers
"that universal mind and . . . the shining tranquillity hidden some-
where behind the colours and the shapes, the pregnant silence
under all sounds, and he thought, 'If one drop of all that ocean

would flow into me now—I know there is something there. I know the sensuous curtain is not a cheat. Help. Help. I want help.' " He had been praying without knowing it.

John's next feeling, according to *Pilgrim's Regress*, is a sense of the terror of the Lord. This terror explains his *reluctance* to accept God: "All things said one word: CAUGHT—Caught into slavery again, to walk warily and on sufferance all his days, never to be alone; never the master of his own soul, to have no privacy. . . ." Then John made this song:

> You rest upon me all my days
> The inevitable Eye
> Dreadful and undeflected as the gaze
> Of some Arabian sky.
> . . . .
> Beating my wings, all ways, within your cage,
> I flutter, but not out.

Earlier it was pointed out that there are two stages in conversion, first the mind, which is intellectual conversion, and secondly the conversion of the imagination and the emotions. *In Pilgrim's Regress* the second stage is reached when the transcendent and distant God of reason becomes personal: *I* becomes *Thou*. God in Christ reaches out to John. This is marked in *Pilgrim's Regress* by John's surprised admission: "You mean I am not my own man. In some sense I have a landlord after all." God is the Landlord. To John, the residence of the Landlord, the castle, seems to threaten him with all the prohibitions of the Ten Commandments. But later he finds that God lives on the Island, which is the symbol of John's longing for the perfection of beauty and love. Reason is satisfied and the personality finds reconciliation and unity. The intellect was satisfied first, and now the inner longing for love is also met.

After coming to believe that the God of the philosophers exists, Lewis had satisfied the demands of reason and conscience, but he had still to discover the Incarnation, the sacrificial and constant love that does not let go. The first stage of Lewis's conversion, however, did have some practical effects, for he began attending College Chapel at Magdalen College, Oxford, where he lectured in English literature, and the eight o'clock service on Sundays at the parish church. (He went to the eight o'clock because he could not stand organ music, and thought it "one long roar.") Each day Lewis read St. John's Gospel in the Greek original, and the practice of reading some portion of the Bible daily he continued for the rest of his life.

Standing in the way of his acceptance of Christianity, Lewis came to see, was intellectual pride. It was self-admiration—posturing all day long, he called it. Many years later when Lewis was asked if he was pleased by his growing fame, he replied: "I shall be careful *not* to think of it!" Prior to his conversion Lewis's first reaction used to be: "Shall I adopt Christianity?" But as his pride was humbled he said: "I now wait to see if it will adopt me. I know there is another Party in the affair—that I am playing Poker, not Patience, as I once supposed."

We must remember that Lewis was a distinguished scholar, a medievalist who also read the recovered myths of Greece and Rome, and the sagas of the Norsemen. So he was inclined to treat the story of Jesus as one more heroic myth in which the hero sacrifices himself. But what finally helped to convince him was the influence of two friends, Dyson and Tolkien, who pointed out to Lewis that when he met the idea of sacrifice in a pagan story he accepted it readily, but denied it in the story of Jesus's crucifixion. Lewis ultimately came to see that the pagan myths were the foreshadowing of the historical truth in the crucifixion, death and resurrection of Christ, the God-man. As a result Lewis's imagination and his emotions were captured, just as his reason had been convinced before.

He recalls the people who had the greatest impact upon him in the following passage from *Surprised by Joy*, where he likens himself to a hunted fox:

The fox had been dislodged from the Hegelian Wood and
was now running in the open . . . bedraggled and weary,
hounds barely a field behind. And nearly everyone
[Lewis respected] was now (one way or another) in the
pack; Plato, Dante, MacDonald, Herbert, Barfield, Tolkien,
Dyson, Joy itself.

It is in two important books that Lewis spells out the importance of satisfying the longing of the heart. One is *Pilgrim's
Regress* and the second is *The Abolition of Man* (1967),
that latter an important address he gave to the National Association of Teachers of English in Schools and Colleges in England.
His essential thesis is that it is the function of great literature,
whether in English or any other language, to keep the imagination
operative; otherwise, he says, we shall live in the flat, measurable
quantitative world of technology, and the imagination will be
starved and the values of religion and morality, which are kept
alive by vision, diminished. In *Surprised by Joy* Lewis indicates
that he would never have been able to return to Christianity if the
great myths in Homer, the *Aeneid*, and the Norse *Edda* had not
kept his imagination alive. Yet there was conflict between the
skeptical intellect and the creative imagination in his schooldays,
which reflects the tension in most university curricula, and Lewis
found that the great danger for religion was a lack of nourishment
by the liberal arts. He feared that the goals of utility and practi-
cality, expressed in vocational training, would soon push liberal
arts out of universities. This was Lewis's position and it is our
dilemma today: "Such then was my position: to care for almost
nothing but the gods and heroes, the Garden of the Hesperides,
Launcelot and the Grail, and to believe in nothing but atoms and
evolution and military service." The dominance of H.G. Wells's
science-fiction in Lewis's youth meant that he was led to believe
in the vastness and coldness of space and the littleness of man.
We may compare Pascal's observation: *Le silence éternel de ces
espaces infinis m'effraie* (I am terrified by the silence of these mea-
sureless emptinesses). It was only the regular reading of W.B. Yeats,
G.K. Chesterton, and George MacDonald, the minister-novelist,
that enabled Lewis to accept Christianity.

The institutional church provided another difficulty. In
Pilgrim's Regress, John is offered help by Mother Kirk early on in
his pilgrimage, but he resists it even though he comes back for her
advice in the end of the book. Lewis disliked clergymen. His
comment on them was: "But though I liked clergymen as I liked
bears, I had as little wish to be in the Church as in the Zoo." His
individualism disliked any form of collectivity, and the "fussy,
time-wasting botheration of it all: the bells, the crowds, the
umbrellas, the notices, the bustle, the perpetual arranging and
organising. Hymns were and are extremely disagreeable to me. Of
all musical instruments I liked and like the organ least."

Lewis was severely criticized by two parties in the Anglican
Church for his satirical treatment of them in *Pilgrim's Regress*.
The Anglo-Catholics strongly objected to their allegorical counterpart, a character named *Neo-Angular*. He was a man who had
little time for the laity, wanted the Church to speak only through
its official spokesmen, had mechanical ideas about the sacraments,
and expressed little charity, being a stiff, stuffed shirt. But the
Liberal Christians—that is, the Broad Church—didn't come off any
better. Their doctrinal beliefs were too indefinite: in fact, they
said, according to Lewis, that doctrine did not matter, only the
religion of the heart. But this was too vague and too indecisive for
Lewis.

Our final consideration will be what Lewis thought of the role
that imagination, which activates the emotions, plays in religion.
For Lewis, Pascal provides the clue in his insight: *Le coeur a ses
raisons que le raison ne connait pas*, "the heart has reasons of its
own of which reason is ignorant." Lewis believed that our lives
are propelled not only by curiosity of an intellectual kind, but by
our desires. It is called *sehnsucht* in German, or "longing" in
English. In the new preface to *Pilgrim's Regress* Lewis explains
that the experience of "intense longing" differs from all other
kinds of longing in two remarkable ways. Though the sense of

want is acute and even painful, yet the mere wanting itself is experienced as a delight. (In this respect it is clearly different from hunger and wanting a good meal—the absence of the meal is not a delight to the gourmet!) Secondly, the object of this desire or intense longing is a mystery. It is not a child's desire for a far-off hillside, nor a desire to be back in the past. It is not reading about romanticism and "perilous seas and faerie lands forlorn," nor an erotic desire for the perfect beloved, nor a love for the occult and the eerie, nor an intellectual craving for knowledge. Lewis says that he has mistaken each of these desires in turn for "intense longing," and has been deluded by each in turn. These desires are not true ecstasy. Lewis has expressed what he has in mind in John's odyssey in *Pilgrim's Regress*, which takes place along a narrow path between the barren rocks of the North country (where the tough-minded humanists who hate romanticism live) and the fetid swamps of the South-lands, where the guides are D.H. Lawrence and Sigmund Freud. It is necessary to walk along a middle path of safety, between resistance to all feelings and acceptance of every feeling.

In his pilgrimage, John makes an important discovery. He finds that traditional morality fails, for without desire or longing it has no motive beyond respectability. Yet desire alone, without morality to restrain it, is equally dangerous. Lewis believes that the ancient myths express the longing in all of us for the loving God who gives himself over to death in order to provide the secret of life. That is the importance of myth, and the universality of myth in every culture, as anthropologists remind us, is the religion that binds the civilization together. But imagination alone will not do. Morality is also needed. Our religious quest is for a master, God, whose threats (commands) become joys, or beatitudes, offering blessedness. So for John and for everyman in his odyssey and pilgrimage there is a search for the Landlord's castle. It is a search for the God who gives the rules and also for the island itself, with its green palms and the cool breezes with the wavelets running along the white sands, symbolizing the fulfillment of desire. Lewis has found a vivid way of indicating that the Christian God is characterized by both law and love, Moses and Christ, Landlord and Lover, or to use Gerard Manley Hopkins's phrase, "lightning and Love." Thus the great saying of Lewis takes on renewed relevance: "God whispers in our pleasures, talks in our conscience, and shouts in our sufferings."

C.S. Lewis's journey to God is in some respects similar to the route taken by Søren Kierkegaard, the Danish philosopher. Kierkegaard had said that first of all we tread the primrose path of aesthetics and find that all lovely things mirror God, yet all things fade and change. Then we tread the philosophical way of reason, until we find that there are more questions than answers in philosophy. Then we try the moral way, until we find that there are many differing moralities and no one has ever succeeded in keeping wholly moral. The stages of Kierkegaard's journey are similar to Lewis's use of reason, imagination, and conscience, which are only to be found in God. For both writers discover that God is unchanging beauty, unchanging truth, and unchanging goodness, and all that we have longed for and found only partially expressed in this world is fully expressed only in God. And C.S. Lewis has proved for many to be a reliable guide to the land that John Bunyan called "the delectable mountains."

ALBERT CAMUS

Christian Ethics Without Its Theology

Albert Camus, the French existentialist novelist, essayist, and playwright who died in 1960, cannot be understood without some grasp of this own particular philosophy, which he called the philosophy of the Absurd. Camus develops this idea of the Absurd in his books of essays, *The Rebel* and *The Myth of Sisyphus*, as well as in two of his novels, *The Stranger* and *The Plague*. Absurdity is a sense of life as marking time in a meaningless and potentially hostile universe.

How does the sense of the absurdity of life arise?

First, it can arise from the nausea we feel at the sheerly mechanical character of everyday life in which we seem to be sleepwalking rather than pulsing with life. So much of living is sheer habit. As Camus describes it in *The Plague*, living is

> getting up, the bus, four hours in the office or factory, lunch, four more hours of work, the bus, a meal, sleep, and monday, tuesday, wednesday, thursday, friday, with the same rhythm, this route is very convenient for most of the time. One day, however, the question, "Why?" is asked and boredom and nausea set it.

A sense of the absurd also arises from the strange and alien character of nature, the primitive hostility of the world in which one knows oneself to be an absolute stranger. What is the sea but Davy Jones's locker? What is the sun, especially in equatorial areas, but a huge bronze and pitiless disc that creates deserts? Typhoons and earthquakes and the glaciers of the ice age that was and will come again treat human beings with no more respect than human beings treat flies.

The sense of the absurdity of life can also come from the feeling that all our days are stupidly subordinated to tomorrow, a dull preparation for a retirement which we may never see, or which, when it arrives, may leave us feeling as useless as a great whale stranded on the seashore. For time itself is the enemy, bringing all our achievements to nothing. By contrast with this sense of the random quality of our life is our knowledge of the certainty and finality of death. Let me quote Camus on this theme: "No morality, no effort are *a priori* justifiable considering the bloody mathematics of our condition." (*Aucune morale, aucun effort ne sont a priori justifiables devant les sanglantes mathématiques de notre condition.*) To make the matter worse, our intelligence that acknowledges its ineptitude or incapacity to understand the world also lets us know that this world is absurd and peopled with irrational beings.

In fact, however, it is not the world that is absurd, but rather the desperate desire of human beings to see the irrationality of the world as rational. The sensible person accepts its absurdity, and Camus depicted such a person in his novel *The Stranger*. This novel, as well as *The Myth of Sisyphus*, appeared in 1942. Meursault, who is the narrator of the novel, is an insignificant office clerk in Algiers. His undramatic existence is ruled by the repetitive requirements of everday life and by the hunt for elementary sensations. For Meursault, daily living takes place in a state of torpor; he cultivates indifference. Although he has not at the start of the narrative achieved a sense of the absurd, he already acts as if life were meaningless. We can divine the absurdity of life in episodes such as his insensitive reactions to the impending death of his mother, and his behavior at her funeral. He does not trouble to mourn her death, and on the day after the burial goes bathing with a former girl friend and takes her to a comic movie. He becomes accidentally involved in a fracas in which he kills a man, and is hauled into prison. His total unconcern for traditional values and conventions scandalizes the lawyers hired to defend him, and he is condemned to death.

Characteristically, Meursault has no interest in the visit of the prison chaplain; he does not believe in God. He remarks that rather than prepare for another life which may not exist, he'd rather spend his last moments concentrating on this life. Meursault enjoys his final hours remembering the past and, in particular, one amorous evening under the stars in a cloudless sky. His great anger finally purges him of evil, and in his last "night of stars and signs" he opens himself "to the tender indifference of the world." In the next to the last sentence of the book Camus reaffirms the absurdity of life and the irrationality of the universe. His hero turns out to be a banal robot, wholly impoverished, convinced that everything in life is a facade, and that behind the facade there is nothing. All he seems to have lost is his own anxiety, but he has lost it at the cost of appearing a somnambulist. His job was routinized insignificance, and his escapes took the form of women, movies, lazing in the midday sun, and drinking an aperitif.

For Camus, to recognize the absurdity of placing one's reliance heavily on the order and rationality of a world that cannot provide either leads to three important consequences. Camus believes that the individual through revolt, through assertion of liberty, and through compassion can by the sole trick of conscience refuse suicide and transform an invitation to death to a rule for life. It is an exhilarating prospect for the young, the healthy, and the independent. Each of these terms—revolt, liberty, and compassion—warrants consideration. To revolt, first of all, is to refuse to find any basis for aspiration or hope in the world. Such a revolt is the acknowledgment of a shattering destiny without the resignation to accept it. The very revolt confers value and grandeur on life, elevates human intelligence, and invites the human race to exhaust itself.

To rejoice in liberty means to throw off the chains of God's or society's laws, and to find freedom in one's self. No longer is one

the slave of mere mechanical habits or of conventional morality.
Ivan Karamazov cried, "All is permitted," but this cry has more
of sadness than joy. Although Camus accepts no standards for
mankind beyond what is human, he does not believe that everything is permitted to the liberated person. Some acts serve and
others debase humanity. An essential part of Camus' thought includes a humanism that accepts as the standards of good and evil
acts that help or hinder men and women.

Camus' philosophy of heroic Stoicism is best exemplified in
his reinterpretation of the ancient Greek myth of Sisyphus, who
was condemned eternally to push a rock to the top of the moun-
tain. As soon as the rock reached the top, it would roll back down
by sheer gravitational pull. He must continue to do this forever,
since the gods had devised for him the worst punishment imagin-
able—the repetition of useless work done without hope. But
Sisyphus makes himself superior to what crushes him. His greatness is achieved through this struggle and in a masterless world he
gains the only happiness possible for human beings. Hence he
becomes the prototypical absurd hero. Camus' retelling of the
myth ends with these words:

> I leave Sisyphus at the bottom of the mountain. He will
> always regain his burden. But Sisyphus teaches the higher
> fidelity which denies the gods, lifts up the rocks. He also
> judges that all is well. This universe in future masterless
> does not seem to him to be either sterile or fertile. Each
> one of the grains in this stone, each mineral glitters in this
> mountain full of night, forms a world alone for him. The
> struggle to the summits is enough to fill the heart of a
> man. We must imagine Sisyphus happy.

Nevertheless, Camus believes, a solitary Sisyphean attitude is
not enough. Compassion is also necessary. In his *Letters to a
German Friend* (published in 1948 but written during the occupation of France, when Camus edited a journal for the French
Resistance) Camus has to refute the theories of his German friend,

who tries to justify the Hitlerian conquest by every means possible on the "all is permitted because the world is absurd" philosophy. Camus replies that he himself has chosen justice in order to remain faithful to the world. He adds that he continues to believe that there is no sense in anything beyond this world, but that something *in* it needs sense; human beings are the only creatures in the world who demand to have it. This view was confirmed in *The Plague* (1947) and in his philosophical essay, *The Rebel* (1951). In the latter Camus puts forward a slogan: *Je me révolte, donc nous sommes.* "I revolt, therefore we exist." Why does a slave revolt, if he does not believe there is something permanent in him, something resembling a soul? The slave believes that in accepting slavery he would deny something that belongs to all human beings, even those who oppress and insult him. We have a collective value which justifies sympathy, community and service to others. Our final aim must be to reduce the misery of the world, although injustice and suffering will continue to exist as long as the world goes on. Thus the true philosophy is *apprendre à vivre et à mourir et pour être homme, refuser d'être dieu*, "to know how to live and to die and to be human, to refuse to be god."

In *The Plague* Camus imagines a severe epidemic of bubonic plague has broken out in the North African town of Oran and we experience the story of the plague through the dispassionate, scientific, neutral terms of a medical doctor's journal, that of Dr. Rieux. So at the first level the novel is a chronicle of the out-break of a disease: the symptoms, the continuing struggle despite setbacks, the hope raised by a new vaccine, the agonies, the burials, and the prophylactic incinerations. At a second level, however, this is the narrative of a man who is both a psychologist and moralist who, with the help of the reports of his friend, Tarrou, analyses the individual reations to the plague. These reactions include egoism, defiance, the pain and the misery of separation, and the fading of one's capacity to visualize the loved ones from whom one is separated. Corporate reactions include escapism in lavish spending or theater-going, blind gropings toward faith, and finally, the learning of the apprenticeship of solidarity. Most profoundly, at the third level, we have an allegory of the evils in our society, the plague of the twentieth century. In this way Camus can give his vision of the world as enemy-occupied territory and the universe as a detainment camp. This anti-topia has foreshadowings of nuclear war, the arrival of the totalitarian state, and a rootless mass culture.

There are five main characters in *The Plague*, and the first to be introduced is Grand—a modest employee of the state, an insignificant and self-effacing character who has a little good will in his heart. He is the kind of man who spends his after-office hours painstakingly writing up the statistics of the plague and uses any spare time in writing the challenging opening sentence of a novel, but never gets to complete that one sentence to his satisfaction. Another character, Rambert, is a Parisian journalist trapped by the epidemic in Oran. He uses all the contacts he has to try to escape illicitly from the besieged city to get back to his mistress in Paris, but he finally decides not to leave the cursed city because, in his own words, "it is possible to be ashamed of being happy all alone"—a fine statement of Camus' belief that to seek happiness only for oneself is to quit the human race and its problems and sufferings.

Father Paneloux, a Roman Catholic priest, is the official representative of Christianity. He tries to reconcile the advent of the plague with the justice of God in a widely attended sermon that interprets the plague as a divine chastisement on the citizens of Oran for their neglect of God. In a later sermon Paneloux affirms his bare faith that one has to assert the role of God in everything, for God is omnipotent or he is nothing.

The two characters who come closest to expressing Camus' own philosophy of life are Tarrou, the intellectual, who though a man in revolt, organizes a group of medical assistants to create isolation wards and thus attempt to delay the further attack of the plague; and Dr. Rieux himself, the inexhaustible adversary of the plague and the one with whom the other four unite to combat the sickness. Rieux's attitude is perfectly expressed in the reasons he gives for keeping a journal of the progress of the plague: "To state simply what one learns in the middle of plagues, what had to be done, and what, doubtless will have to be done again, against terror and its tireless arm, despite their personal wounds, for all men who, unable to be saints and refusing to admit plagues, force themselves all the same to be doctors." The most impressive achievement of all is the fraternity that develops in a struggle without hope, a resistance movement of the spirit motivated by compassion.

One way of reading the novel is to examine the various interpretations of the plague itself that are put forward by the characters. Father Paneloux, the Jesuit father, is cast in the role of "official" Christian interpreter. When the plague is at its height, the local authorities decide to have a week of prayer climaxed by a high mass in the town's cathedral under the patronage of St. Roch, the saint who protects against plague, with Paneloux as the preacher and a huge congregation attending.

Paneloux's sermon begins in a rather striking fashion because it begins so bluntly: "Calamity has come on you, my brethren, and, my brethren, you deserved it." He went on to say that the first time this scourge appeared in history, in Pharoah's Egypt,

> it was wielded to strike down the enemies of God. Pharoah
> set himself up against the Divine will and the plague beat
> him to his knees. Thus from the dawn of history the
> scourge of God has humbled the proud of heart and laid
> low those who hardened themselves against Him. Ponder
> this well, my friends, and fall on your knees.

Next Paneloux uses a metaphor in which the world is the threshing floor and the plague is God's flail to separate the wheat from the chaff. All the people present may have assumed that they would

in time repent, counting on God's compassion and patience, but
God tired of waiting: "the same pestilence which is slaying you
is working for your good and points your path." Finally, Paneloux expresses in the sermon the hope that "despite all the horrors
of these dark days, despite the groans of men and women in
agony, our fellow citizens would offer up to heaven that one
prayer which is truly Christian, a prayer of love. And God would
see to the rest."

Therefore Paneloux is using a theological rationale—God
chastising his impious people—in order to make some sense out of
plague, and render the events susceptible to reason by placing
them in a context people can understand. The other point of view
is represented by the agnostic physician, Dr. Rieux, for whom the
evil constitutes a scandal, an injustice irreconcilable with the idea
of God as good and all-powerful. The encounter between the
differing points of view is shown most vividly when the doctor and
the priest spend the night at the bedside of the dying child of
M. Othon, the governor of Oran. Both are horrified by the apparently useless suffering of this child, "pouring out the angry death-
cry that has sounded through the ages of mankind." Paneloux
sinks upon his knees and hears Rieux say in a voice hoarse but
clearly audible across that agonising, never-ending wail: "My God,
spare this child!"

As the tired Dr. Rieux turns to leave, Paneloux says to him,
"Why was there that anger in your voice just now? What we'd
been seeing was as unbearable to me as it was to you." Rieux
turned towards Paneloux. "I know. I'm sorry. But weariness is
a kind of madness. And there are times when the only feeling I
have is one of mad revolt."

"I understand," Paneloux said in a low voice "That sort
of thing is revolting because it passes our human understanding. But perhaps we should love what we cannot
understand." Rieux shook his head at Paneloux.
"No, Father. I've a very different idea of love. And

until my dying day I shall refuse to love a scheme of
things in which children are put to torture." A shade of
disquietude crossed the priest's face. "Ah, doctor," he
said sadly, "I've just realized what is meant by 'grace.' "

Paneloux delivers his second and humbler sermon at a mass
held especially for the men of the town. Now he is no longer a
detached observer, for he has become one of those who faces
death day after day as a member of Dr. Rieux's team out fighting
the plague. The church is three-quarters full largely because
superstition has usurped the place of religion, with prophylactic
medals of St. Roch and prophecies of Nostradamus. Father
Paneloux says that he stands by what he had said in his first
sermon, but perhaps it had lacked much charity. All trials, he
argues, work well for the Christian and we should, despite
appearances, discern both good and evil. What baffles us is
apparently needless suffering, the horror it inspires in us, and the
reasons we must find to account for it. In other manifestations
of life God makes things easy for us, and to that degree our religion has no merit. But in this respect God has put us, so to speak,
with our backs to the wall. He would not use the usual simple
devices such as the argument that a child's sufferings, for example,
would be compensated for by an eternity of bliss. Paneloux's
hearers must practice the virtue of total faith. Since the suffering
of the child was part of God's will, we too should will it. Thus the
Christian would be forced to accept everything so as not to deny
everything. "The sufferings of children [are] our bread of afflic-
tion, but without this bread our souls would die of spiritual hunger."
The choice is either to hate God or to love him, and who could
choose to hate him? "My brothers, the love of God is a hard love.
It demands total self-surrender, disdain of our human personality.
And yet it alone can reconcile us to the suffering and the deaths
of children, it alone can justify them, since we cannot understand
them, and we can only make God's will ours. This is the hard
lesson I would share with you today. That is the faith, cruel in
men's eyes, crucial in God's, which we must ever strive to
compass."

Thus Paneloux's version of Christianity stakes everything on faith in the trustworthiness of God and in the next life's rectification of the injustices of this life, and the meaning of life is to live compassionately by faith, by hope and in charity. Camus rejects the hope of a future life, yet he has a tremendous urge for compassion and a remarkable trust and faith in humanity.

Some idea of Camus' own faith is given in two sections of *The Plague*. One is in a very interesting discussion that goes on between the two friends, Rieux and Tarrou, the doctor and the intellectual; the other is found in the very final paragraph of the novel.

At their first meeting, Tarrow finds inexplicable the devotion from which springs Dr. Rieux's dedication to improve the lot of the sufferers. "Why do you yourself show such devotion, considering you don't believe in God?" Some minutes later Rieux replies, "Since the order of the world is shaped by death, mightn't it be better for God if we refuse to believe in Him and struggle with all our might against death, without raising our eyes toward the heaven where He sits in silence?"

At a much later meeting, Tarrou confesses that he has had a kind of conversion to humanism, owing to his recognition that society creates its own criminals and that the establishment concurs with injustice. "For many years I've been ashamed, morally ashamed, of having been, even with the best intentions, even at many removes, a murderer in my turn . . . I have realized that we all have plague, and I have lost my peace."

Rieux asks Tarrou, what is his path for attaining peace? Tarrou replies that his path is empathy with all who suffer and an attempt to alleviate suffering.

"It comes to this," Tarrou said almost casually. "What interests me is learning how to become a saint."

"But you don't believe in God."

"Exactly, can one be a saint without God? That's the problem, in fact the only problem I'm up against today."

Several minutes later Rieux replies, "But, you know, I feel more fellowship with the defeated than with the saints. Heroism and sanctity don't really appeal to me, I imagine. What interests me is being a man."

The other place where Camus' realistic philosophy comes out clearest is at the very end of the novel. The plague is now over, but

> Rieux remembered that such joy is always imperilled. He knew what those jubilant crowds did not know but could have learned from books: that the plague bacillus never dies or disappears for good; that it can lie dormant for years and years in furniture and linen-chests; that it bides its time in bedrooms, cellars, trunks, and bookshelves; and that perhaps the day would come when, for the bane and the enlightening of men, it would rouse up its rats again and send them forth to die in the happy city.

Although Camus was baptized a Roman Catholic and received his first communion, it was after only two years of inadequate catechetical instruction. His widowed mother was not a believer and his uncle fueled the anti-clericalism of the public schools by encouraging him to read Voltaire and the atheistic *philosophes* of the eighteenth century. Furthermore, his first teacher of philosophy, Grenier, preferred Hinduism to the God of the Christians. His grandmother was a Christian, but his friends were not; it was natural that he should come to associate Christian faith with wrinkles, immobility, and the loneliness of the aged.

Camus has three main indictments of Christian theology.
First, it seems to him a totalitarian form of belief. Jean Onimus,
in his admirable book *Albert Camus and Christianity*, cites an
instance where Camus compares the total allegiance demanded by
Christianity to the partial claims of the Greek gods: "The Greeks
did not deny the gods, but they did allocate to them their share.
Christianity, which is a total religion, cannot admit this attitude."
For Camus, Christianity clearly suffers from this comparison. *The
Rebel* insists that Christianity breaks the will to revolt, counseling
acceptance of the human lot: "For a human mind there can only
be two possible universes, that of the sacred (or, in the language of
Christianity, of grace) and that of revolt."

Camus' second criticism of Christianity is that it devalues the
earth and postpones all that gives worth to this present life to an
invisible future. By contrast Camus is the celebrant of the
ephemeral, of that which is transient, passing. He believes that
Christians have invented another world at the expense of this one,
and he loved to quote the dictum of the poet Alfred de Vigny:
"Love what one will never see twice." Christians, he maintains,
will always be displaced persons on this earth because they seek a
heavenly city.

Camus' third major objection to Christianity, the most powerful in his mind, is the way in which it tries to gloss over the power
of evil. The dilemma from which Camus could not escape was the
following: either God does not exist and the world is absurd, or God
does exist and it is he who is evil. This view is firmly expressed by
Dr. Rieux in his reflection that it is better for God that human
beings do not believe in him and continue struggling against death
with all their might, rather than look to heaven where God sits
silent. Camus even claims that the crucifix on Catholic altars portrays a martyred innocent and therefore symbolizes the omni-
potence of evil. What reply can Christians make to these charges?

Jean Onimus has argued in his book on Camus' religion that
Camus gets his understanding of Christian theology from St.

Augustine, as well as from Søren Kierkegaard and Blaise Pascal.
Certainly Camus loathed the rigidity with which Augustine condemned unbaptized infants to damnation. He seemed to be better
acquainted with Kierkegaard and Pascal, who have been considered Christian existentialists. It is significant, however, that both
religious philosophers did battle with the rationalists of their day,
who diluted the Christian faith with secular humanism. Thus
they were left with the austere and distant God of the philosophers, rather than with a holy but loving presence. Camus' God
is a hidden God and a tyrant, never the loving father of a prodigal
son. So Camus' mutilated faith issued in a humanistic revolt.

It can be argued that in order to have faith in the world, one is
required to have faith in God; it is not surprising then that ultimately Camus had no faith in the world. Camus' alternative is an
ulcerated humanism, for he has given up all illusions in technocratic or Marxist man. Yet there are glimmers of what might have
been in Camus' longing for an absolute to trust, and, in his last
novel, *The Fall*, even a nostalgia for innocence.

The final question Camus must be asked is this: Is life a
terminus or a tunnel? For Camus it is a terminus: death is a high
and insuperable wall, the ultimate absurdity. To believe that
death is a tunnel, leading through darkness to ultimate light, is
the hope that Christians have but one which was excluded for him.
The only purpose of the endless struggle that is life is, for Camus,
to continue it. It is a more heroic concept of life than that of the
Christian, but also a more doomed and hopeless view—it may
satisfy the secular saints among us, the few superior stoics who
will face the firing squad. But the majority of us must feel like
King Edwin's thanes and advisers that the Venerable Bede writes
about in his *History of the English People*. When asked to be
advised whether these preachers of the South who had come from
Rome with good tidings were to be listened to, one of the king's
advisers replied: "The life of man, O king, is like that of a bird
that enters into one window, is seen for a moment in the light of
the fire and then flies out of another window. Where we come

from we do not know; where we go to we do not know. If we can learn something more certain, then let us welcome it." What Edwin and his people learned was the good news of God whose Son had returned from the no man's land of death and who had solemnly promised his followers of every age: "In my Father's House are many mansions; if it were not so, I would have told you. I go to prepare a place for you, so that where I am you may be also."

If one cannot accept the truth of these promises, then the compassionate ethics of Camus and his heroic fight against limitless odds provide the next best view of life. But if one would live with hope rather than against hope, if one would combine a trust in God's love and its ability to challenge and change humanity, with such hope, and a compassion like Camus', then the ancient Christian triad of faith, hope and love, is the greatest of philosophies. Camus's ethics stress compassion, certainly, but they lack faith and hope, and above all, the divine empowerment of grace to enable men and women to become what they wish to be.

GRAHAM GREENE AND FRANÇOIS MAURIAC

Treasure in Earthen Vessels

The glory of the Incarnation of the Son of God is that this grace was revealed in squalor. The glory of the church of Christ is revealed when its priests, ministers and laity are motivated by love for the loveless, when they are seeking amid the tarnished coinage for the image of God in which we are created. St. Paul knew this when he marvelled at the Incarnation and the servants of the Incarnation, and wrote:

> Seeing it is God who said, Light shall shine out of darkness, who shined in our hearts to give the light of the knowledge of the glory of God in the face of Jesus Christ. But we have this treasure in earthen vessels, that the exceeding greatness of the power may be of God and not of ourselves (2 Cor. 4:6-8).

The staggering fact about the Gospel is that light does shine out of darkness and that God's love is known in the miscarriage of justice and in the cross—the instrument of torture is God's sign of salvation. Similarly, his truest servants are human beings, not perfect but with clay feet, in whom the glory of grace shines, treasure in earthen vessels. This is what Graham Greene in *The Power and the Glory* is going to show us in the story of the whisky priest, who fathered an illegitimate child but is still God's witness and martyr in formerly atheistic Mexico. Similarly, François Mauriac in *A Woman of the Pharisees* will show us a priest in the abbé Calou, ejected from the seminary in which he was a distinguished professor, exiled to an insignificant country parish, and even refused the last privilege of celebrating the sacrament of the Eucharist because the "woman of the Pharisees" has reported him to the archbishop. Greene's priest has no discipline and Mauriac's no tact; they lack pride, they are utterly empty-handed, and they are the instruments of the grace of God.

For each author the leading character seems to say: "The proof that the grace is of God is that I am no hero! Don't look at me, look at God; if he cares for me, he surely cares for you, too! We have this treasure in earthen vessels." But it is equally important to notice that they do not say, "Let us sin that grace may abound." Or, "Let's make the clay even earthier, that the treasure may show up by contrast." No, they are aware of the clay and deeply ashamed of it, but amazed that the gracious God uses their ministries.

What is so striking about the novels of Roman Catholic artists, be they Bernanos, Greene, Mauriac, or Guareschi in his Don Camillo series, is their recognition that the Christian is against the world and thought to be a fool by worldlings. Here, again, they are in the true theological succession. St. Paul writes,

> We are fools for Christ's sake . . . being reviled, we bless; being persecuted, we endure; being defamed, we entreat; we are made as the filth of the world, the off-scourings of all things until now (1 Cor. 4:9-13).

Here St. Paul is in the authentic succession of Jesus Christ, for one of Christ's beatitudes includes a realistic promise. "Blessed are ye when men shall reproach you, and persecute you, and say all manner of evil against you falsely for my sake. Rejoice and be exceeding glad: for great is your reward in heaven." (Matt. 5:11-12). The reward is in heaven, not on earth. It is characteristic of great fictional accounts of Christians that they scorn the scorn of the world. Oliver Goldsmith's *The Vicar of Wakefield* portrays a very gullible, but very lovable Dr. Primrose. Fielding's novel *Joseph Andrews* includes a clergyman of integrity who is inevitably thought simple because he lacks shrewdness. And Dostoyevsky in *The Brothers Karamazov* shows us in Father Zossima and Alyosha two more characters who are naive and ingenuous because they love with Christ's love, without counting the cost. In similar ways Bernanos, Greene, and Mauriac emphasize that the true followers of Christ must count the world well lost. Nothing is harder; yet, by grace, the impossible gradually becomes possible. The country priest of Bernanos comes to love the haughty countess who despises him; the abbé Calou of Mauriac comes to love the wealthy Pharisee, Brigitte Pian, who hates him; and the whisky priest learns to love the despised and the bitter, as God loves him. Thus by grace the all-too-ordinary becomes extraordinary. In each case God's witness is a fool for Christ's sake.

A second feature is common to the interpretations of Greene and Mauriac. For both writers, God is the inexorable hunter who will never give up his human prey, but ceaselessly searches it out. For Graham Greene, God is inescapable justice; for Mauriac, both inescapable and compassionate justice. Greene's characters think, like a modern Jonah, they can escape the claims of God, but Greene's God will get even with them at the end. Death is the noose that God draws tight over the would-be refugee from justice. This conviction is what gives such power to his study of the juvenile delinquent, Pinkie, in the book *Brighton Rock*. He may escape the police, but not hell. The same theme of the powerlessness of escape runs through almost all Greene's novels. When the whisky priest has just reached the frontier leading out of Mexico to freedom, destiny in the form of his own conscience drives him back again to the land where death is the penalty for acknowledging Christ. Because he is God's "marked man," he is also the police's "wanted man." Mauriac has the same haunting sense of God as the invisible hunter, and, in fact, defines the priest as "the unbaying beagle who goes before the Divine hunter" to track mortals down. Mauriac subscribes to St. Augustine's view that man will always be unhappy in the dodges by which he tries ineffectually to escape God, whether they be sensuality or pride of the intellect, for "our heart is restless until it finds its rest in Thee." Indeed, part of Mauriac's genius is in seeing that God grapples with the human soul to wrest it from its master passions of human sexuality and covetousness, both of which are forms of pride. Greene and Mauriac both believe that those who try to break the laws of God will instead be broken by them. Both writers also subscribe to the Augustinian view that human beings

will find true happiness only in the bondage of Christian obedience, and that it is only an illusion that they are truly free in
licentiousness. The authors differ in their understanding of that
obedience; for Mauriac, God is compassionate justice, and it is his
love that is the other side of justice. For Greene, God is absolute
justice: there is little sense of the divine love in his writings. Holiness is seen only as a terribly demanding justice, not as love, so
contrary is it to the deepest human desires.

As might be expected, both authors also share a profound
belief in original sin—the recognition that this is a fallen world.
Many of Mauriac's novels show that what is called romance, and
its attendant affairs of the heart, are after all rather tawdry. He
looks behind the facade of fading beauty—the face-packs, the
ominous wrinkles, the sagging body, the furtive encounters, the
flattery that cannot face the truth. It is as if Mauriac is saying,
"Love can only find its lasting loyalty in response to the divine
love for the loveless, this is an unfading love that will not let you
go." And no one can excel Graham Greene in describing and
evoking the lost innocence of the world. Everywhere in his novels
there are symbols of decay and decadence. In *The Heart of the
Matter* we encounter peeling walls, spiders, cockroaches which are
pinned against the wall by slippers thrown at them to mark
intervals in boredom. In *Brighton Rock* a former resort for
English aristocrats and Regency bucks has become a smaller Coney
Island, with one-night cheap hotels, and beaches on which the
masses can drop their litter of potato crisps, candy-rock, and ice-
cream wrappers. There are the artificial fairy-lights on the pier,
the flashy neon-lit hotels, depicting a forced and gaudy sensual
joy. In Mexico the prevailing decadence is captured in symbols
like the vultures waiting to hasten death, the golden-toothed
smiles which enable seedy dentists to make a living by disguising
decay, the harsh superstitions of the Indians bearing testimony to
a degenerate Christianity, and the ominous ruins of past civiliza-
tions that proclaim all our boasting to be ineffectual. The authors
mean to be cruel at first, that they may afterwards be kind. Exposing man's false loves, they hope to turn him to his true love, God.

Another perspective Mauriac and Greene have in common is the notion that it is only our self-love and respectability which blind us from seeing the loveableness of others. To see other human beings as ugly, that is, not to recognize and acknowledge your kinship with them in the human race, is a failure of the imagination. This sense of charity is supernatural, God-given. It is awakened in the whisky-priest when he is put in the town prison for possessing illicit liquor. In this one-chamber jail, there are also a pious woman and two poor young lovers. The pharisaic woman criticizes the hole-in-the-corner lovers and the priest replies: "Saints talk about the beauty of suffering. Well, we are not saints, you and I. Suffering to us is just ugly. Stench and crowding and pain. *That* is beautiful in that corner—to them." "Hate," Greene says, is "only a failure of the imagination."

Abbé Calou in *A Woman of the Pharisees* has the same gift. One of the most exciting moments in the novel comes when the brilliant boy whom the abbé looks after escapes from the presbytery to go and visit his mother; he believes that she, in her wayward way, is very attached to him. He goes to her hotel, several miles distant, and climbs up to her bedroom window, hoping to surprise her with his devotion. As he looks through the window unseen the son finds her with a middle-aged Parisian actor, and is bitterly disillusioned that her lover is so tawdry. The boy tells Calou that he is disgusted that his mother could have fallen for a middle-aged roué, with bulging paunch, dyed hair, and a greedy, grimacing mouth. But the abbé replies: "You must tell yourself that in her eyes he represents wit, genius, elegance. To love another person is to see a miracle of beauty which is invisible to the rest of the world."

This brings me to another link of common interpretation between these two novelists. Each one knows that every true disciple of Christ must reenact the Passion in his own life: "If any man would be my disciple, let him take up his cross and follow me." The deepest unity with Christ is found in suffering, where pierced hand grips pierced hand. The abbé Calou meditates,

'One can always suffer for others'. . . . Then he muttered
as though to himself, 'Do I really believe that? . . . Yes,
I do. What an appalling doctrine it is that acts count for
nothing, that no man can gain merit for himself or for
those whom he loves. All through the centuries Christians have believed that the humble crosses to which they
were nailed on the right hand and left hand of Our Lord
meant something for their own redemption of those they
loved. And then Calvin came and took away that hope.
But I have never lost it.'

Calou knows that the true Christian must be despised and rejected,
but without hopes of becoming a Messiah. His life is a living testimony to Christ's words at Gethsemane, "Not my will, but Thine
be done." Calou's humility is never feigned; he sees himself as
"God's very useless, nay, his sometimes actively interfering
servant." When he is refused the final consolation of celebrating
the Mass, the abbé records this meditation in his diary,

'I now stand in the presence of my God, as naked, as
much stripped of all merit, as utterly defenseless
as a man can well be. Perhaps it is the state in which
those of us should be whose profession it is . . . to be
virtuous. It is almost inevitable that the professionally
virtuous should hold exaggerated ideas of the importance
of their actions, that they should constitute themselves the
judges of their own progress in excellence, that, measuring
themselves by the standards of those around them, they
should be made slightly giddy by the spectacle of their own
merits.'

This humility, with which Calou recognizes the world's verdict
by scorning himself, is linked with a profound sense of pity and
forgiveness. The word from the cross speaks to him: "Father,
forgive them, they know not what they do." Calou understands
that every soul is unique and different and must find its own way

to God. There are no well-marked or easy paths to God, but each must pursue his own circuitous route. As Calou himself says to Brigitte Pian, his persecutor,

> 'Each one of us has peculiar destiny, and it is perhaps one of the secrets of the compassionate justice which watches over us, that there is no universally valid law by which human beings are to be assessed. Every man inherits his own past. For that he is to be pitied, because he carries through life a load made up of the sins and merits of his forbears to an extent which it is beyond our power to grasp. He is free to say yes or no when God's love is offered to him, but which of us can claim the right to judge what it is that influences his choice?'

In such pity, in such humility, in such forgiveness, Calou walks the way of the cross and wins for God the soul of the woman of the Pharisees. For she is transformed by the forgiveness of Christ that is manifested in his servant. The Abbé Calou is despised, rejected, but at last he has been accepted.

Graham Greene's *The Power and the Glory* also forces his priest to tread the way of the cross. Both Catholics and Protestants would allow that the Holy Communion is a reenactment of the sacrifice of the cross. Greene's whisky priest celebrates the sacrament at first as a rather meaningless rite, though its celebration gives him his prestige. And he is doing rather handsomely out of it, as the fact that he is growing stout shows. A frequent guest at baptismal parties and weddings, it is ironical that he celebrates the sacrament of the altar that was death to Christ and is a means of livelihood to him. Soon, however, as Mexico becomes officially an atheistic state, to celebrate the Mass becomes a dangerous occupation. In the end the whisky priest becomes himself a sacrificial victim, an image of the sacrifice of the Mass itself. As the flesh of Christ was torn and his precious blood poured out on the cross, so is the flesh of the whisky priest broken by the firing-party and spattered against the wall. He is now a martyr. The genuine apostolical succession is found in those who wear the visible or invisible stigmata.

A fifth factor common to the interpretation of these Catholic novelists is one of universal significance. They both contrast a false piety, which is the expression of a religion of self-glorification, with a true devotion to Christ that expresses a piety seeking glory for God and for others. Greene shows us the self-importance of pious people in the following conversation between the priest, who is hearing the confessions of the whole village in the early hours before dawn, and a garrulous woman who has come to the confessional. The priest says, abruptly,

> 'I'm not interested in your fish-supply or in how sleepy
> you are at night. . . . Remember your real sins.' 'But
> I'm a good woman, father,' she squeaked at him in
> astonishment.
> 'Then what are you doing here keeping away the bad
> people?' He said: 'Have you any love for anyone but
> yourself?' 'I love God, father,' she said haughtily. He took
> a quick look at her in the light of the candle burning on
> the floor—the hard old raisin eyes under the black shawl—
> another of the pious like himself.

The superb finish of *The Power and the Glory* derives its whole point from the contrast between the cardboard, melodramatic idea of a martyr saint, and the reality of the man who died for Christ, almost apologizing before he collapsed as a corpse before the firing squad. A pious Catholic mother is telling her children that they have a new saint and martyr in Mexico. "Yes," she says, "he was one of the martyrs of the Chruch." "He had a funny smell," one of the little girls said. "You must never say that again," the mother said. "He may be one of the saints." The boy wonders if anyone managed to soak some of the martyr's blood in a handkerchief. The mother replies: "I think if your father will give me a little money, I shall be able to get a relic."

"Does it cost money?" "How else can it be managed? Everyone can't have a piece." Here you have the selfish side of piety, the exploitation of saintliness for one's own benefit, as contrasted with the greatest of the martyrs, Christ himself, who died for everyone.

Similarly, one could say that the whole theme of Mauriac's novel, *A Woman of the Pharisees*, lies in the contrast between the Pharisaism of Brigitte Pian and the genuine piety of the abbé Calou, which is Christ-centered and other-centered and very rarely self-centered. The novel is concerned with unfolding the subtle self-deception of the Pharisee. She abounds in good works by which she hopes to merit salvation and she always, in distributing her monies, lets her right hand know what her left hand is doing. Even worse, she dominates and exploits others by her charities, making them her dependents. We see this in her treatment of the schoolmaster, Monsieur Puybaraud, who has been thinking about asceticism and the priesthood as his vocation. He has, however, come to feel a deep love for a simple Christian woman, whom he marries. When his wife dies in childbirth, Brigitte Pian implies that this is the divine judgment on his sexuality, despite the fact that she herself remained a widow for only a few months. She also tries her utmost to destroy the love of her ward and step-daughter, Michèle, for the independent young aristocrat, Jean de Mirbel. Pian would, indeed, have succeeded but for the abbé Calou's determination that her interference shall not succeed, and it costs the abbé his right to remain as a priest in the village. For masquerading beneath this piety is the iron will of a woman who assumes that whatever her will dictates is the divine will; hers is the crushing possessiveness of a boa-constrictor that suffocates the freedom of all who are her dependents.

To mark the contrast, Mauriac lavishes all his sublety in making the abbé Calou the instrument of grace, as by his humility, his forgiveness, his deep pity, he struggles to win her soul with a selfless charity. He possesses the terrible meekness of truth, the loving truth, which sees through all illusions. He is a remarkable character study. Calou is never shocked by the stratagems of evil, but continually marvels that God can win any contests of grace with men. He can see others with the imagination of Christ's vision. It is his mediation of forgiveness that wins the woman of the Pharisees in the end and transforms her. This religious master-piece ends with the following words:

> In the evening of her life, Brigitte Pian had come to the knowledge that it is useless to play the part of a proud servitor eager to impress his master by a show of readi-ness to repay his debts to the last farthing. It had been revealed to her that our Father does not ask us to give a scrupulous account of what merits we claim. She under-stood that it is not deserts that matter but our love.

The true witness of God is motivated not by reputation, but by love. That is how a false is distinguished from a true piety.

So, in summary, we may see that in six very important issues, Greene and Mauriac agree in their religious interpretation of reality.

A Christian must be—in the world's eyes—a fool for Christ's sake.

God inevitably either takes his captive or leaves him profound-ly dissatisfied, for the function of the 'invisible hunter' is to drive the soul out of the thickets of illusion—intellectual pride, sensual-ity, or greed for possessions—into the open where he will discover that in Christ's will is his peace.

Apart from the acceptance of Christ as the way and the truth and the life this is a lost world, where innocence has disappeared.

The pursuit of the truth in Christ is bound to bring suffering, but this is the closest identification we can have with the strange man on the cross.

Having Christ, we can recognize all other souls not as ugly (our pride only thinks that) but rather as potentially beautiful, for they are the souls for whom he died.

Finally, true saints and true piety never advertise themselves; that is the sign of false piety. Truly pious men and women are oblivious of self, and live for God and other people. Here is the most brilliant of all Greene's insights: the the saint is not aware of it! The true saint is merely an anonymous instrument in God's hands. In these six common factors we have six reasons for asserting that Greene and Mauriac are profound religious novelists and interpreters of the God who is "lightning and love."

There are, of course, differences between the two novelists in terms of their technique. It is easy to see that Mauriac writes the leisurely psychological novel in which the French excel, delving into motivation and character with the subtlety of a surgeon laying aside first the skin and then the flesh to reach the beating heart. A gesture, a parting look, an expression—all these are meaningful to a novelist like Mauriac. By contrast, Greene's novels are almost all variations on the technique used in mysteries —breathtaking escapes and pursuits, where the dialogue is stream-lined, reading almost like connected telegrams, and the action is quick as a derringer. Mauriac deserves his Nobel Prize, for his talent and workmanship are consistently masterly, but in one respect Greene is his superior. No one has more subtly brought the apocalyptic dimension into religious writing. In secular writing, of course, you can find it already in the novels and stories of Franz Kafka, but Greene gives his novels the backcloth of heaven and hell and shows that actions have abiding consequences. Who but Greene, in the heyday of liberalism in the Thirties, would have dared to report this conversation between Pinkie, the young gangster, and Rosie, his girlfriend?

(Pinkie) 'I don't take any stock in religion.
Hell—it's just there. You don't need to think of it—before
you die.
'You might die sudden.
He closed his eyes beneath the bright, empty arch, and
memory floated up imperfectly into speech.
'You know what they say—'Between the stirrup and the
ground, he something sought, and something found.'
'Mercy.
'That's right. Mercy.
'It would be awful though,' she said slowly, 'If they didn't
give you time.' She turned her cheek onto the chalk
towards him and added, 'That's what I always pray. That
I don't die sudden.
'I don't,' he said.

A similar concern is expressed in *The Heart of the Matter*,
where Scobie's great problem is whether to accompany his wife
to Mass despite the fact that he has not been able to go to confession to admit his adultery. Thus Scobie is willing, in order to
hurt neither his wife nor his mistress, to lose his immortal soul.
And Graham Greene, it seems to me, is really asking whether
Scobie's love, which will damn itself for others, is not greater
than the limited confines of the Church's love for souls, or
whether it is an expression of the ultimate weakness? For Greene,
the present life is always viewed against the background of
eternity.

Perhaps what makes one of the novels we have been considering, *The Power and the Glory*, so important for Greene, and
vibrant with vitality and urgency, is its prophecy of a world (on
whose edge we are living) where Christianity will again become a
forbidden faith, as it was in the days when the Roman Christians
could only gather in the underground caves of the catacombs or
cemeteries, a world where God will be more of a hidden presence
than he is today, and Christians will be a secret sect. For Greene

believes that the atheism he saw as a reporter in 1938 in Mexico, and described in *The Lawless Roads*, is a dress rehearsal for the coming atheism of all Europe, as official atheism is today the dominant belief of much of Asia. This eschatological urgency Francois Mauriac has recognized as the chief quality of Greene. Mauriac writes,

> The power and the glory of the Father burst forth in the Mexican curate who loves alcohol too much and who gets one of his parishioners pregnant. A type so common and mediocre that his mortal sins call forth only derision and a shrugging of the shoulders and he knows it. What this extraordinary book shows us, if I dare say so, is the utilization of sin by grace.

He goes on to mention the apocalyptic dimension in Greene:

> We feel it is that hidden presence of God in an atheistic world, that subterranean flowing of Grace which dazzles Graham Greene much more than the majestic facade which the temporal Church still erects above the peoples. If there is a Christian whom the crumbling of the visible Church would not disturb, it is, indeed that Graham Greene whom I heard at Brussels, evoking before thousands of Belgian Catholics, and in the presence of a dreaming apostolic nuncio, the last Pope of a totally dechristianized Europe, standing in line at the commissary, dressed in spotted gabardine, and holding in his hand, on which still shone the Fisherman's ring, a cardboard valise.

Greene lets us see the new church of the catacombs as it will come again, shorn of political power but strong with the power of Christ's own dedication in her. In *The Power and the Glory*, God is everywhere visible only to the acute eyes of faith.

For Greene, grace is always a strange visitant in the squalor of
this world in which it makes its temporary home. God's servant is
the stranger introduced into the dentist's waiting-room at the end
of the novel. He is simply God's black question mark, a symbol
of hidden grace beneath the squalor of shabby clothes and ethics.
Grace is hidden, like the holy medal beneath a man's shirt found
on one of the prisoners. Even books of piety can only be
smuggled into Mexico if they have glossy covers, as if they were
pornography. Even the priest himself is an earthen vessel, so
much so that it is only with difficulty that the treasure of the
gospel in him can be revealed bit by bit. It is because he can see
virtue in others, sympathize with and forgive others, but see no
virtue or reason for forgiving himself, that the whisky priest has
plumbed the depths of humility. Like those of the abbé Calou,
his hands are empty. Because he has no human pride or possessions to cling to, he is ready to receive the riches of God's grace.

Both *The Power and the Glory* and *A Woman of the Pharisees*
are filled with Christian insights, as I have tried to demonstrate.
The grace of God and the squalor of the Church needing reforma-
tion are ultimately two arguments for a deeper commitment to
the ongoing Christian life. Ultimately, they are the only two
arguments for joining the Church, and both are St. Paul's. The
Church cost the very life blood of Christ, and Christ needs prophetic souls to help make it what it should be. In the Church we find
grace, and its squalor is a challenge to transform the Church into
God's intention for it. The apostle to the Gentiles said, "Christ
loved the Church and gave himself for it"—the first argument and
the greatest—"that He might present to Himself without spot or
wrinkle, or blemish, or any such thing"—the second argument.
In presenting these claims so vividly, our novelists have been faithful to their religious as well as to their high artistic calling.

GRAHAM GREENE'S THEOLOGICAL THRILLER

The Power and the Glory

Two valuable clues to the meaning of *The Power and the Glory* are given by its alternative titles. The American title, dropped in subsequent impressions and editions, was *The Labyrinthine Ways*. The title recalled the admirable poem, "The Hound of Heaven," written by another English convert to Catholicism, Francis Thompson, with the key opening stanza speaking of the soul evading God the hunter:

> I fled Him down the nights and down the days
> I fled Him down the arches of the years,
> I fled Him down the labyrinthine ways
>   Of my own mind, and in the midst of tears
> I hid from Him . . . .

It is a story of a runaway from God who is finally persuaded to return to him, as the prophet Jonah was. Jesus, too, spoke of God's loving search for the lost sheep in a parable—the Good Shepherd leaves the ninety-nine sheep in the fold so that he might search out and discover the errant sheep and protect it from the wolves. Jesus's own definition of his mission was, "The Son of Man came to seek and to save that which was lost" (Lk. 9:10).

The English title under which the book appeared, *The Power and the Glory*, is appropriate for two reasons. On the one hand it shows that the real glory of God is seen in his martyrs who witness to him by their deaths. On the other hand, Greene may be pointing out that the pomp and circumstance of the Roman Catholic church, with its pontifical masses at which the white-robed Pope presides in Rome on great occasions, its splendid cathedrals like St. Peter's in Rome with the sculpture of Michelangelo's Pieta and the ornate Solomonic twisted pillars over the high altar and the chair of Peter designed by Bernini, is a great departure from the simplicity of Christ, who was buried in a borrowed grave. The power of the Church can rather be seen in the fidelity of the poor Mexicans in the novel, who risk their lives in an atheistic state in order to adore Christ in the Mass, and in their very ordinary priest who becomes extraordinary by grace at the last. These reflect the ending of the Lord's Prayer: "For Thine is the Kingdom, the Power, and the Glory for ever."

The brilliance of this novel lies in its depiction of a double hunt. Its protagonist, the whisky priest, is the marked man for the police in the persecutions of the church in Mexico, as it was in the early forties of this century. But he is also God's marked man, his elect, his chosen. Paradoxically, the priest is chosen and marked for death, as a traitor to the state and as a Christian martyr in the world. Even more mysteriously, God's marked man tries to evade both police and God at first. He seeks to escape God "down the labyrinthine ways of *his* own mind, and in the midst of tears, *he* hid from Him . . ." Thus *The Power and the Glory* is a stunning theological thriller.

Greene's preparation for writing this novel was two-fold. He had already become a writer of mystery novels, such as *The Man Within* (1929) and another eschatological thriller called *Brighton Rock* (1938) in which the destinations of heaven and hell are clearly a factor in the story of Pinkie, a juvenile delinquent. An equally important preliminary was the writing of a study of Mexico, which Greene was commissioned to prepare, entitled *The Lawless Roads* (1939). There he describes how the Catholic church in Mexico was persecuted in certain provinces, and how, although religious services were forbidden, the people continued in secret to worship the God they were prohibited from worshipping publicly. Greene believed that in an increasingly secular world, with the growth of totalitarian regimes, whether Communist, Nazi or Fascist, Mexico was a forecast of what would happen in other parts of the world. Such an outcome would mean for the Church a new scarlet flood of martyr's blood poured out. Hence the apocalyptic urgency with which he writes, and its relevance for those to whom faith is important. Unlike other visitors to Mexico, Greene did not condemn the fussy Baroque candlesticks, and the dressed-up and doll-like statues of the Virgin as over-dramatic, illusionistic art. He thought that after the drabness, monotony, and colorlessness of the peasants' lives, they deserved every element of beauty and drama their religion could provide. He describes the Templo del Carmen in San Louis sympathetically:

> The Virgin sat on an extraordinary silver cloud like a cabbage with the Infant in her arms above the altar; all along the walls horrifying statues with musty purple robes stood in glass coffins; and yet it was home. One knew what was going on. Old men came plodding in in dungarees and bare feet, tired out with work, and again I thought: how could one grudge them the gaudy splendor of the giltwork, the incense, the distant immaculate figure on the cloud? The candles were lit, and suddenly little electric lights sprayed out all over the Virgin's head. Even if it were all untrue and there was no God, surely life was happier with the enormous supernatural promise than with the petty social fulfillment, the tiny passion and the machine-made furniture.

In addition, Greene was humbled by the way the exhausted poor peasants were ready, after a day's back-breaking work, to undertake mortification in their worship, where at Mass

> the peasants kneel in their blue dungarees, and hold out their arms, minute after minute, in the attitude of crucifixion; an old woman struggles on her knees up the stone floor towards the altar; another lies full length with her forehead on the stones . . . . This is the atmosphere of the *stigmata*, and you realize suddenly that perhaps *this* is the population of heaven.

Greene was to make the towns of Tabasco, where every church was
destroyed, and Chiapas, where the Mass was forbidden, the vivid
background of his novel.

The primary theme of *The Power and the Glory* is *deus
absconditus*, the hidden presence of God in an unbelieving world.
In Mexico we again witness the early church of the catacombs.
All triumphalism has vanished. The true Church is invisible, and
the distinction between the conventionally pious and the true
disciples of Christ is known to God alone. The disciples know
that the last on earth shall be the first in heaven, and their mark
is the inward and invisible badge of entering into the fellowship of
Christ's sufferings. In its Mexican form this new church of the
catacombs meets only in mud huts. Packing cases form the altar.
The chalice of communion is a chipped cup; the wafer a hard
crust. Confessions are hastily recited, only allowing time for
mentioning the important sins truly regretted. And the Mass, far
from being a conventional rite, is a true communion between
Christ and his own, in which both priest and people risk their
lives to keep the faith. Although this Church lacks temporal
power, it has the power of an increasing dependence upon God,
not human beings, and manifests an increasing self-denying
charity, and a new humility and simplicity.

In these circumstances God is visible only to the eyes of
faith, which can penetrate spiritual reality behind material
phenomena, and tear off the masks with which men and women
disguise their desires as necessities. The stranger introduced in
the dentist's waiting room, the "black question-mark," is in fact
a priest, a symbol of hidden grace beneath the shabbiness of
clothes *and* character. The stranger who knocks at the door at
the end of the novel, when it seems that all priests of integrity in
Mexico are dead, reveals himself as another man of God in
unclerical and ordinary garb. The apostolic succession continues,
even if outwardly it is unimpressive. Holy medals are now forbidden, so the symbol of Christian loyalty is worn under the
shirt. As in the burying places of imperial Rome, Christians are

once again known by a secret sign. Even books of piety can only be smuggled through the customs if they resemble glossy-covered pornography. The whisky priest himself, formerly plump and pampered as in the newspaper photograph taken shortly after his ordination, now wears torn peon's pants and tattered shirt, while his chin exhibits unshaven stubble and his skin is blotched and bleeding; he is God's man disguised as a criminal. This man, no longer conscious of any moral superiority, who yet believes in the basic goodness of everyone but himself, is an earthly symbol of what Gerard Manley Hopkins, following St. Thomas Aquinas, called the Catholic Mass, namely, "Godhead here in hiding."

Even the officials of the atheistic state are aware of a God-shaped blank in the mind and in the space-time context of human life. Their desperate desire to wipe out all records of Christianity is witness to a concealed deity. Thus an Anti-God Museum in its iconoclastic determination is unintentionally a sign of God. This sense is subtly conveyed by Greene in the ensuing passage:

> The lieutenant walked home through the shuttered town. All his life had lain here: the Syndicate of Workers and Peasants had once been a school. He had helped wipe out that unhappy memory. The whole town was changed: the cement playground up the hill near the cemetary where iron swings stood . . . like gallows in the moony darkness was the site of the cathedral. The new children would have new memories; nothing would be ever as it was. There was something of a priest in his intent observant walk—a theologian going back over the errors of the past to destroy them again.

The paradox of God's hidden presence in the state is revealed strikingly through the priest. He is rejected by the atheist society as a traitor, who, when he is apprehended, will be liquidated without trial. He is also elected by God to be his witness in life and especially his martyr in death. He is, oddly enough, an alcoholic priest who with the appropriate formula is believed

to be able to transform wine into the blood of Christ, the medicine of immortality. Through a symbolic correspondence, the
wine that he imbibes is transformed by the grace of God into
blood that will eventually be shed for the love of Christ. He is the
father of an illegitimate child, and yet is addressed as a spiritual
"father" by the tribute of the faithful. One who would not have
been surprised by this paradox is St. Paul, for it was he who
wrote: "We have this treasure in earthen vessels, that the exceeding greatness of the power may be of God, and not from ourselves" (2 Cor. 4:7).

The treasure is of course the gospel of God's grace, and the
casket in which it is contained is God's human minister. The very
shabbiness of the habit and habits of the priest is a safeguard
against idolatry. He is the better able to be God's marked man
because he is the police's wanted man. Ultimately Greene shows
us that the saint unawares is the true saint, the one who attributes
all failures to the disregard of grace and all successes to God.

The second theme in Greene's novel is the human need for
redemption from original sin. We live in a warped world, in
which innocence is lost and where Nature and human nature are
crude, perverse, and violent. Human beings are egocentric and
lustful, and in desperate need of grace. No one can compare
with Greene in his use of the symbols of decadence, whereby the
environment is literally falling into decay. The disintegrating
roads are eroded by the unsurping jungle and by tropical floods
and storms. Vultures and buzzards waiting for their carrion meals
of wounded or dying men and beasts watch alertly. Snakes slither
through the undergrowth; they evoke memories of the Garden of
Eden, where the original sin was committed. Greene depicts the
violent cruelty of blood oozing out of a dead Indian baby, shot by
the police because an American gangster used it as a hostage with
which to shield his stomach. We see decadence not only in the
superstitions of the Indians, but also in the yellowing, aged eyes
of the *mestizo* and his carious fangs of ochre color. It is seen in
the raisin-like eyes of the pious woman at the confessional, who

wants heaven only for herself. Everywhere the mark of imperfection and finitude, of death and decay, frustration and failure, mars the world. And for those who lack the purpose faith provides, life is as meaningless as that of the black beetles that explode against the walls in such prolific waste, and as irritating as the mosquitoes that sound like endlessly turning sewing machines.

For the lieutenant of police the world is orphaned, and entropic. Greene says of him,

> It infuriated him to think that there were still people in the State who believed in a loving and merciful God. There are mystics who are said to have experienced God directly. He was a mystic, too—and what he had experienced was vacancy—a complete certainty in the experience of a dying, cooling world, of human beings who had evolved from animals for no purpose at all. He knew.

Padre José, who has married and given up the priesthood, also believes in an orphaned universe. It was easy for him to give up asceticism, for with the change in the political regime he renounced his Orders. He is only irritated by the ironical reference to his past when the children of the neighborhood mocked him by repeating in the high-pitched accents of his bony wife, *come to bed, José*! The whisky priest, however, believes that this is a world visited by God, to which God had come in the flesh in the Incarnation of Jesus Christ, and that he comes again at every renewal of the Mass. So for him it can not be an abandoned world.

In this world of lost innocence, our status is no longer a little lower than the angels, but only just above that of the animals. One is impressed, rereading this novel, by the frequency of animal images that Greene uses to indicate a drop in human status. For example, the former priest José's wife "fed him and fattened him and preserved him like a prize boar." Later, Greene describes his "little pink eyes like those of a pig conscious of the slaughter

room." Captain Fellowes, a minor character in the novel, sings
vacuously about the snouts of trouts as he chugs through the
banana plantation in his motorized canoe, and a "monkey made a
sudden chatter at him as he went by, and Captain Fellowes felt
happily at one with nature—a wide shallow kinship with all the
world moved through his veins." One feels that he is closer than
he should be to his simian ancestry. In Greene's world, men are
egged on by the primal instincts of hunger and lust, like the animals, yet they are more than the animals because they are made in
the image of God, whose reason and will are still operative. Even
former temptations become tedious; men become jaded even in
their lusts, like José, who begins to hiccup with nerves at the
thought of facing his harsh housekeeper wife—"She would be in
the big shameless bed that filled up half the room, a bony shadow
in the mosquito tent, a lanky jaw and a short grey pigtail and an
absurd bonnet."

Inevitably, the third theme in Greene's novel must be the
recovery of integrity—the purging of guilt and the action of grace
lifting the weight of guilt from the soul, whose disability is
described by St. Augustine as *incurvatus in se*, "twisted in on
itself." The third theme is the most important, for it shows how
the divine hunter and lover tracks down the fugitive man, as God
tracked down Jonah, brought Augustine to himself after embrac-
ing philosophical alternatives and life styles, captured C.S. Lewis
by an inexpungable longing, and found the Franciscan nuns ship-
wrecked off the coast of England who were commemorated by
Hopkins in "The Wreck of the Deutschland." God is not only
hunter and lover, but also the sharp physician of souls; his probing
scalpel and sharp knife are cruel in order to be kind, because
through suffering he cuts out the egocentric cancer of the soul.
That is his way with Greene's whisky priest, for Greene knew as
well as Flannery O'Connor did that if God cannot win by love, he
will terrify by the anger of lightning; if he cannot melt by affection, he will freeze the rebel soul. This love of God is inexorable
and relentless, refusing to abandon its victim; in Francois
Mauriac's marvelous definition of the priest, *il marche devant*

comme le chien du Chasseur invisible, "he goes in front like the hound of the invisible Hunter."

For Greene, the grace that offers new life is objective; it is utterly independent of the unworthiness of the human agent meditating upon it, precisely because it is divine grace and un-merited. The great strength of the saints is that they who are ordinary become extraordinary through grace. And the grace or generosity of God, as a Protestant would define it, is especially vivid in squalor. This is exactly what makes the Crucifixion so magnificently relevant, as it is a love which goes as far as death for the undeserving. The whisky priest meditates on how often he had

> heard the same confession. Man was so limited: he hadn't the ingenuity to invent a new vice: the animals knew as much. It was for this world that Christ died. The more evil you saw and heard about you, the greater glory lay around the death; it was easy to die for what was good or beautiful, for home, or children, or a civilization—it needed a God to die for the half-hearted and the corrupt.

Greene shows us that the acceptance or rejection of grace has apocalyptic dimensions, for the choice offers two alternative and ultimate destinations, heaven or hell. It is the eternal significance of human choices that gives the Christian saga as interpreted by Greene such weight and depth; the flat world of humanism has become three-dimensional, just as in the course of the novel Greene shows us the maturation of grace in the life of the whisky priest. We watch the sparks of the divine love, or grace, grow into a fire of blazing charity. Its manifestations become increasingly impressive. The priest comes to love his hard-faced, bitter child Brigida, for whom he prays, "O God, give me any kind of death—without contrition, in a state of sin—only save the child." He also realizes that he should, as a priest, love all God's children like his own. He manages even to appreciate the lieutenant of police, his enemy and eventual executioner, for his prayer, "Excuse," is surely a Christ-like prayer for his enemies. The same marvelous *caritas* is revealed when the priest rebukes those in the jail with him who criticize a young couple making love in a corner, and he reminds these pious people that hate is "a failure of the imagination." Again, when a woman in the confessional before Mass only talks about her virtues, the priest asks her what she is doing among sinners if she is so perfect, and inquires where her love of God is, defining "love" here as the desire to protect God from one's self. The priest looks everywhere for the very image of God in humanity, no matter how spotted it may be. All pride has been burnt out in him as he comes to a genuine, not a postured, humility.

His closer identification with Christ is revealed in his brief conversation with the half-caste who lures him back into Mexico that he may receive the confession of the American gangster before giving him the *viaticum*. The half-caste pleads,

'He's dying and you and I wouldn't like to have on our conscience what that man . . . .'
(Priest) 'We shall be lucky if we haven't worse.'
(Half-caste) 'What do you mean, Father?'
(Priest) 'He's only killed and robbed. He hasn't betrayed his friends.'
(Half-caste) 'Holy mother of God, I've never . . . .'
(Priest) 'We both have.'

It is at this point that we recognize that the priest is reenacting the sufferings of Christ in his own life, and this is his betrayal which will lead thereafter to his death as martyrdom.

An important fourth theme of the novel makes the point that St. Augustine had to emphasize with his rigorist and unforgiving opponents, the Donatists, who argued that the moral shortcomings of priests prevented them from being channels of the grace of God in the sacraments. The book ends with the whisky priest dying and believing himself to be the last legitimate priest in Mexico, and in his place another "black question-mark" arrives to continue the work of God. It is significant that neither the whisky priest nor his successor is given a name; they do not figure as personalities, but are merely instruments in the hands of God. The ordinary become extraordinary through the suffering that is borne by grace, and it is these ordinary saints who maintain the labyrinthine tasks of the hidden but providential God in a world which appears abandoned. The generations come and go, but the task of the priest is to seek persistently the holy love of God and to mediate his grace in all human relationships. Despite the priest's inadequacies, God is never defeated.

Greene's novel has been criticized on many accounts. He is thought to have a religious vision that includes producing divine grace like a rabbit out of a hat, and its workings are thought to be too unpredictable and miraculous. How could so ordinary, morally shabby a character as the whisky priest, who had fornicated once and was frequently drunk, become so extraordinary as to die a martyr? The New Testament, however, portrays Saul of Tarsus as a determined persecutor of the church who by grace became the apostle to the Gentiles, and cowardly Peter on the day of crucifixion became the chief apostle to the Jews, and, according to early Christian tradition, both died as martyrs. To expect martyrs to be of their own achievement people of outstanding courage is to be a Pelagian. Greene therefore glorifies God's grace in his servants, not their own powers. A Catholic answer might also stress that this Church has never underemphasized the miracle and mystery of God's ways.

Greene has also been criticized for having a very sour view of human nature. Whether this is a fair judgment or not, depends on whether one is a liberal humanist or whether one has a religious point of view and consequently believes that humanity is sick and needs divine aid. It might more fairly be argued that devilry rather than divinity dominates the novels of Greene. This is how he sees

the world, and Greene insists that "perfect goodness walked the
earth only once." In comparison with the perfect integrity of
Christ, all human deeds are gray or black. Greene's creed seems to
be, "I suffer, therefore I am." But here again after the bland views
of optimists, it is a relief to find a more realistic approach, even
if it occasionally seems pessimistic and lacking in joy. More justified is the view that Greene has a grossly inadequate view of
human sexuality. He seems to regard the act of love as dirty,
degrading, furtive, and shameful, under any circumstances, as
citations from *The Heart of the Matter, England Made Me, Brighton Rock,* as well as *The Power and the Glory* would readily
demonstrate. One may surmise that he is even less hopeful about
human love than St. Paul, who claimed that marriage was only
slightly better than continuing to burn with lust; even St. Paul
used marriage as the metaphor for the bond between Jesus and his
body the church. Yet even this criticism must be qualified by the
tender love that radiates the chill in *Dr. Fischer or the Geneva
Bomb Plot.* Perhaps the truth is that Greene claims human beings
are made in the image of God, as he shows in the previously mentioned prison scene, but more often he is overwhelmed by the
squalor of human lust. Here is a typical passage:

> God is the parent, but his image dangles from a gibbet, or
> in the camel act of sex. God is the parent but his progeny
> are the policeman, the maniac, the priest.

The balance of Christian realism is achieved in affirming that
human beings can be redeemed.

In conclusion, for all its seedy vividness Greene's vision is
myopic. He is so blinded by the evil of the world that there are
extremely few glimpses of the sunshine and warmth of grace in
his work. Human love is seen only as a betrayal of the love of
God, and in the crudest possible terms. Greene's theological interpretation lacks the necessary balance between sin and grace,
between human beings as crucifiers and as creatures who can be
redeemed. It is as though Greene's version of the Gospel ended

with the Crucifixion, ignoring the Resurrection and the descent of the Holy Spirit at Pentecost. Greene's vision is too one-sided to be true. Far better as a summary of faith is the title of Frederick Buechner's Lyman Beecher lectures, *Telling the Truth: the Gospel as Tragedy, Comedy, and the Fairy Tale that is True*. For the Christian it is a tragi-comedy, not an unrelieved tragedy.

WILLIAM GOLDING'S *SPIRE*

Three Interpretations

The most discerning critics value William Golding highly. Arthur Koestler avers that he has come "as an earthquake in the petrified forests of the English novel," while Kingsley Amis acclaims him as an artist combining the "utmost inventiveness, assurance, and power." John Davenport asserts that Golding has "Wellsian powers of creative imagination and a strictly disciplined style" and insists that he is "the most purely original English novelist of the last decade." These judgments are those of novelists writing about a competitor!

There are two outstanding qualities in Golding's fiction. One is the extraordinary differences in the scenarios of his novels in both space and time, and the other is his intense seriousness as a fabulist, a creator of fables, in his interpretations of human life and destiny. Both points may be briefly illustrated. And not the least interest in studying Golding is the varied possibilities he offers for interpreting his message.

His first novel, *Lord of the Flies* (1955), starts off with a group of choirboys marooned on a Pacific island. *The Inheritors*, published the same year, transports the readers to the prehistoric caves where Neanderthal man lives. *Pincher Martin* (1956) has as its protagonist a naval officer on a destroyer that is torpedoed in mid-Atlantic and casts him up as a survivor onto a barren rock, or so he imagines. Part of the locale of *Free Fall* (1959) is a German military prison, while *The Spire* (1964) is a novel about the building of the spire of Salisbury Cathedral in England during the fourteenth century. Golding can hardly be accused of repeating himself in time or space.

He is also a fabulist, or writer of parables, with multiple levels of meaning. *Lord of the Flies* is an analysis of the danger of atavistic tendencies that lie beneath a thin veneer of education and civilization. *The Inheritors* concerns itself with the lost innocence of the race and the corruption of Neanderthal primitives by the cunning of the "new people"—the humans. *Pincher Martin* is about hell, the sphere in which a man of absolute greed lives in isolation, alienation, and utter egocentricity of spirit, as befits a character who "was born with his mouth and his fly open and both hands out to grab." *Free Fall* is the story of Sammy Mountjoy, a character whose existence seems utterly without a pattern or purpose, his search for a pattern, and the two options he finds —the one rationalist and the other religious. The unifying theme in interpretations of these novels lies in their recognition of the reality of the Christian ideas of the Fall and of original sin, of human sinfulness as a prerequisite to redemption.

My chief concern in this essay is with the differing ways in which Golding's novel, *The Spire*, can be interpreted. Perhaps the most attractive feature of this novel is the fact that it is a paradigm of the author's way of writing a novel. The theme is Dean Jocelin's vision of a glorious spire topping his cathedral of Salisbury in southern England, a spire that will be four hundred feet high, and how this vision is to be brought about. In each novel Golding has a central interpretative idea, and the problem is how he is both to turn it into narrative and to make its meaning reveal itself. Jocelin is opposed by everyone in the pursuit of his vision, including Anselm the sacristan and all his fellow members of the cathedral chapter. The building project endangers the congregation because the foundations of the tower on which the spire will rest are rotten and marshy, and eventually it has to be moved elsewhere, and thus the whole purpose of a cathedral, the corporate adoration of God by his people, has to be suspended. The lives of the master-builder and his men are also dangerously threatened. Jocelin clings to his dream despite all the opposition, which he believes to be both human and demonic.

This very subtle book could be interpreted as a struggle to the death between vision and faith on the one hand, and dogged

common sense on the other. The dean would then be symbolic
of the profound faith that goes on believing in God's power
even though the foundations are insecure, since God is the ultimate foundation of all human life. The spire will be kept in place,
despite all the swaying of the winds and the singing of the over-
stressed pillars that seem to cringe as they support it, by a "holy
nail" from Christ's cross. If one followed this interpretation one
could explain the novel as an affirmation of the unimportance of
the objections of rational men, who can see no further than the
ends of their noses. For them the conception of a miracle, which
is the objective counterpart to faith, is utterly unthinkable.

In actual fact the struggle is much subtler. The master-builder,
Roger, is earthy enough, with his lust for Goody Pangall and his
tolerance for his men's ridicule of Goody's lame and impotent
husband. And mingled with Jocelin's design to glorify God in
this superb spire are other ambitions less exalted. There is his
own ambition, which is symbolized by the four images of his pro-
file he intends to have carved on the tower supporting the spire,
his ruthless indifference to the unhappiness of his goddaughter
Goody Pangall, in whose womb grows the ungodly seed of Roger
the master-builder, and his conviction that the spire is a perfect
diagram and symbol of prayer, which is at the same time belied
by his refusal to waste time on worship in the cathedral. The
dean also forces the master builder to construct the tower on
insecure foundations to greater and greater heights, although
Roger suffers from vertigo, and he is indifferent to the casualties
caused by the building. He appoints Ivo, an illiterate hunter, a
canon in the cathedral simply because Ivo had provided the
necessary wood for the scaffolding of the spire and tower.
Finally, there is the brutal fact that the money for extending the
house of God heavenwards came from Jocelin's aunt, who gained
Jocelin his promotion while acting as the king's mistress. So at
the outset it appears as if Golding is asking two basic questions,
and the first is, what place is there for the seraphic logic of faith
in a world in which authoritative knowledge is scientific? Although the setting is the fourteenth century, the question itself
is tantalizingly modern. The second question has to do with the
mixed nature of human motives. Are not even saints all-too-
human persons with tremendous will power aided by grace?

How are we to decode the symbol of the spire? It is a symbol with polyvalent possibilities. On the lowest and most naturalistic level we may ask: How did the medieval builders manage to thrust their huge towers, high glass-skinned walls, and sky-piercing spires ever upwards? By modern standards these builders were scandalously unconcerned about their foundations. Peterborough Cathedral was built upon a peat bog. The central tower of Carlisle hangs above two small streams. Wells Cathedral is surrounded by pools. Ely's Norman tower fell in 1322, providing the opportunity to replace it with the delicate octagon of Alan of Walsingham. Beauvais in France was built too high, with the resultant collapse of the vaulting. Chichester's cathedral spire fell in 1861, the walls buckling and bending during Christmas services and tumbling into the nave in February. Building a spire was at best a very risky matter, and from a strictly functional point of view quite unnecessary. The cathedral that Golding knew best, since he had been an English teacher at the grammar school there, was that of the town of Salisbury, England's loveliest and highest. This cathedral was built in 1330 to the height of four hundred feet, and since it rises from a marshy subsoil, its erection seemed to be an act of supreme daring or doltishness. In the first few years it settled twenty-three inches out of true, and six hundred years later the engineers are still worried by it.

Yet while there is an element of naturalism or realism in Golding's fable, that element does not provide the primary meaning. Can we get at this meaning by discovering what the spire means as a symbol? Like the cathedral itself, the spire is in the first place the symbol of a miracle. When the master-builder digs beneath the crossing of the nave to discover what foundations exist to support the new tower and the tall spire, the following conversation takes place between Roger and Dean Jocelin:

The Dean: 'Confess, my son. I told you the building was a miracle and you would not believe me. Now your eyes have seen.'
Roger: 'Seen what?'

The Dean: 'A miracle. You've seen the foundations; or,
rather, the lack of them.'
The Dean adds later: 'You'll see how I shall thrust you
upward by my will. It's God's will in this business.'

The spire is also a phallic symbol; it is a failing spire, an
expression of impotence. This use of symbolism is indicated by
the novelist's description of the model of the spire:

The model was like a man lying on his back. The nave
was his legs placed together, the transepts on either side
were his arms outspread. The choir was his body; and
the Lady Chapel where now the services would be held,
was his head. And now also, springing, projecting,
bursting, erupting from the heart of the building, there
was its crown and majesty, the new spire.

In terms of the book's sexual symbolism, the spire might also
suggest the compensation for celibacy which Jocelin finds in his
bawdy dreams of Goody Pangall, the goddaughter whom he has
married off to impotent Pangall the watchman. In the ironic and
ambiguous ending of the novel, when Jocelin is on the verge of
death and those at his bedside are trying to persuade him to make
an act of faith preparatory to receiving the last sacrament, the
only word the weakened man can frame is, "Berenice." The
saintly Father Adam at his bedside assumes Jocelin is invoking the
aid of a saint. It is more likely, however, that the dean is thinking
of "Berenice's Hair," a constellation of stars, and so of the stream-
ing and seductive hair of Goody Pangall, and of the spire among
the stars. The spire is both a visionary and a sexual symbol, as
is human experience—a compound of innocence and guilt.

In the third place, the spire could be viewed as a symbol of
aspiration, a diagram for prayer. Dean Jocelin, as the building
becomes more difficult, tries to explain to Roger the significance
of the spire. "My son, the building is a diagram of prayer; and
our spire will be a diagram of the highest prayer of all. God

revealed it to me in a vision, his unprofitable servant. He chose me. He chooses you, to fill the diagram with glass and iron and stone, since the children of men require a thing to look at."

Furthermore the spire is a symbol of the inexorable and terrible demands of the divine will. Dean Jocelin is speaking: "When such a work is ordained, it is put into the mind of man. That's a terrible thing. I'm only learning now how terrible it is. It's a refiner's fire . . . You and I were chosen to do this thing together. It's a great glory. I see now it'll destroy us, of course."

Finally, and more subtly, the spire is a very ambiguous symbol of Jocelin's folly and above all a symbol of his faith—the faith that God can do the impossible. This is superbly expressed in the following soliloquy of the Dean:

> And the folly isn't mine. It's God's Folly. Men can do that for themselves. They can buy and sell, heal and govern. But then out of some deep place comes the command to do what makes no sense at all—to build a ship on dry land; to sit among the dunghills; to marry a whore; to set their son on the altar of sacrifice. Then, if men have faith a new thing comes.

Thus we have exemplified one favorite method of exegesis, the interpretation of a novel through its powerful and imaginative symbols.

A second method of interpretation is that suggested by Wesley Kort, an able expositor of religion in fiction at Duke University. He argues that *The Spire* should be analyzed in terms of its plot rather than in terms of its images. The plot is essentially structured upon the change in the situation of Dean Jocelin during the course of the novel. The plot has three parts, each consisting of four chapters, and these parts correspond to stages in the construction of the spire. The first part deals extensively with the preparations for the building, especially the excavation of the pit to determine the strength of the foundations. The second part deals with the building of the tower and the spire. The third and last part shows the completion of the spire and how it remains standing.

Early on in the novel we gather that the desire to build the spire is the consequence of a vision granted to Jocelin. However it is soon evident that there is no respectable foundation for the work, since the money to maintain the work is to come from Jocelin's aunt, the king's mistress, who wants to be buried in the odor of sanctity. There is no popular support for the spire; ultimately, Jocelin is its only supporter. When the workmen dig to find a foundation, they discover none. Instead of the rock they hoped to find, there is only a stinking pit of decay and death. This is Golding's inimitable description of Jocelin's first sight of the bottom of the pit:

> He saw one [pebble] stir, as with a sudden restlessness; and then he saw that they were all moving more or less, with a slow stirring, like the stirring of grubs. The earth was moving under the grubs, urging them this way and that, like porridge coming to boil in the pot . . . Some form of life; that which ought not to be seen or touched, the darkness under the earth, turning, seething, coming to boil . . . Doomsday coming up; or the roof of hell down there. Perhaps the damned stirring, or the noseless men turning over and thrusting up; or the living, pagan earth, unbound at last and waking, Dia Mater.

The problem of the foundationless spire is made worse by the emotional strain the spire will impose on the people of the church, as well as the physical stress on the architecture. Instead of acting as their chief pastor, Jocelin will now exploit his flock. He ignores the ironic, raucous laugh of Rachel, Roger's wife, and the flirtation beginning between Roger and Goody Pangall. At this time

the pillars are, like the entire life of the church, under tension
and strain.

The middle section of the book, which centers on the raising
of the tower and spire, is a painful time for Jocelin, a time of both
joy and guilt, faith and risk, in his inner life. He is as happy as a
sandboy in the tower, but he also experiences guilt when the
workmen begin to quit because they are horrified at his arrogance
in building so high without supporting foundations. Roger the
master-builder drinks to cover his fear, a fear compounded by
vertigo and guilt. The church suspends its worship. All ethical
values are given up; religious considerations predominate. As
Roger takes the risk of building too high, Jocelin risks common
sense and his own popularity through his faith that with God all
things are possible. The higher the spire ascends, the higher is the
risk of faith and the greater the strain. Jocelin senses the strain
as he feels the sheer weight of the stone, the swaying of the tower
in the wind, and the singing or screaming of the pillars, and the
threatened heaviness of the capstone with the cross at its acme.

In the final four chapters the anxiety of building is over, and
Jocelin receives the hurtful truth through the offices of his chaplain, Father Adam, and his old friend the sacristan, Father Anselm.
He is made to realize his sin and his stupidity. He is removed from
his position as Dean, and he also loses his life. Having given birth
to the spire, he dies, like Goody Pangall. Jocelin stands revealed
neither as a saint nor a pathetic figure, but as a Sophoclean tragic
hero. His flaw is not idolatrous pride, but his own ignorance and
limitations. A really commanding figure, he has great will power
and also great weakness.

How can this "interpretation" be interpreted? Kort's is a
humanistic interpretation, downplaying all the theological clues,
but still very original. Kort's own words of explanation are,

What the book celebrates, I think, is that arising out of,
accompanied by, and resulting in human stupidity,

sin, and sickness, is this glorious spire, this triumph which
is its own excuse for being. Out of the mud, the blood,
the sin and the slime, we have this "new thing" . . . .
From the tower of Babel and Prometheus down to our
own arts and sciences, we recognize how poorly the
human enterprise is based. Still, though creation drains
a man, falls on his head, or reduces him to itself, it
stands, if only for a while. And that moment of standing
is the precious point of Golding's groundless spire.

A third intriguing interpretation is a Biblical and theological
one. David Anderson, in his lively book *The Tragic Protest*,
claims that *The Spire* must be interpreted as Golding's version of
the legend of the Tower of Babel. The eleventh chapter of
Genesis provides us with a story in which all men combine to
build a tower that will reach up to heaven. This story illustrates
the energy, enterprise, audacity, and endless self-confidence of
human beings, whose imagination transcends their context and
their contemporaneity. This is human glory and nobility, the
aspiration to overcome one's environment. Thus the tower of
Babel, in the opinion of its builders, reveals them at their supreme
best, distinct and superior in planning and execution to all other
forms of sentient life.

In exactly the same way, Jocelin conceives of his spire as the
ultimate prayer. Although the spire will only be four hundred
feet from the ground, its aspiration will reach to eternity. The
builders of the Tower of Babel were unable to complete their
work. The Lord came down, and confused their languages, so
that they were unable to understand each other. The narrative
was intended, says Anderson, as an explanation of how the single
human race came to have so many different languages. More
significantly, however, the story can also be read as a parable of
the inability of the proud to meet in agreement. It may be that
as the tower grew higher, there was a series of disputes about the

design, and doubts as to the adequacy of the foundations to
support the increasing weight, as in Golding's novel. There might
have been discussion as to the suitability and strength of the
materials. Then, also, as the work became harder and required
more heroism, the builders might have lost faith in the worth-
whileness of the task. Labor troubles might have ensued: discussions of the dangers increasing with the height, and disagreements
about wage scales. What is made clear from the Biblical account,
however, is the sense that the work stopped because the builders
had overreached themselves. Hence the paradox of human nature:
we are aware of the claims of the Absolute, but we respond to
these claims of the Holy Spirit only partially and relatively, in an
unholy manner. We catch a glimpse of the towers of eternity
partly hidden by the mists of time and space that engulf us, and
our fairest or most ambitious dreams are unattainable because
we are human beings, not God. Thus Babel is a parable of frustration—man-made bridges and towers crack and crumble; the enduring bridge must be built by God.

Jocelin's spire is built, but it is twisted and far from safe; it
affirms the imperfections of human achievement. Jocelin has
forced the spire up against reason and flesh, yet he believes that
in doing so he serves God. We question human attainment at its
highest because of the mixed nature of human motives. Anderson writes,

> We do not really require a doctrine to tell us that man
> is prone to violence and barbarism, because that is only
> too obvious; what we do need is a doctrine which ques-
> tions our noblest aims and reminds us of the mingling of
> evil with good in the best of our actions.

There is *hubris*, infernal pride, in Jocelin's claim that the spire
is wholly the work of the Holy Spirit. Equally distorted by pride
is Jocelin's view of Goody Pangall as a witch sent to pollute his
spirituality by her involvement in birth, death, and sexuality.
Hence Anderson interprets *The Spire* finally as an expression of

Golding's belief that a Manichean dualism, attempting in the interest of the spirit to demolish the claims of the flesh, is unacceptable to God and destructive of human being. The irony of this attempt to escape from the raptures and ruptures of the flesh into a state of exalted spiritual beatitude on the part of Jocelin is that the building of the spire was only made possible by the sins of the flesh. His aunt, Lady Alison, paid for the cathedral with her body. So also did Goody Pangall with hers, for she kept Roger Mason at work for love of her. So the spire is not pinned to the sky by the holy nail, as Jocelin claims, but owes its existence to human corruption and perversity.

What is one to make of this third interpretation? Its strength lies in its Biblical basis and its recognition that the greatest human sin is pride, the pride of Titanism that wished to be as God, as St. Augustine so brilliantly defines it in his *Confessions*. For those who prefer a theological to a humanistic interpretation, it has the advantage of basing itself on the symbol of the Tower of Babel as a primeval example of overweening pride. In one respect, however, both Wesley Kort and David Anderson seem to have overlooked a most important symbol near the end of the book. Unquestionably both see the inherent and corrupt sickness in Jocelin's pride, although they may not term it original sin. But both ignore the scene where in the cloister garden Jocelin is delighted by the sight of a glorious blooming apple tree that ascends like a white waterfall in reverse—symbolizing the grace brought by the new Adam, Christ, from Paradise.

Finally, then, the delight of Golding's masterly work is the divergent ways in which it can be interpreted. You can explain it in theological or humanistic terms, in terms of its images or in terms of its plot. You can take it as a parable of stoicism, or of the limits of the human condition and the necessity for divine grace at the beginning and the end of life, or you can see it as a parable of the Tower of Babel in modern guise. And nothing better illustrates the enigmatic, ironic, and ambiguous quality of our author than the concluding, if inconclusive, end of the novel.

On his death bed Jocelin's mind is wandering, thinking of kingfishers and apple trees, not of matters of sanctity. Father Adam,
waiting at his bedside with the Host, hopes to hear some word of
faith or assent. Leaning down,

> he saw a tremor of the lips that might be interpreted as a
> cry of *God! God! God!* So of the charity to which he had
> access, he laid the Host on the dead man's tongue.

Was that a triple calling on God, an invocation of the Holy
Trinity? Or was it a curse? Was it a terrible cry of fear as the fog
of death clutched the throat? And was Father Adam's charity
justified in the case of Jocelin? And since the Host was placed on
the dead man's tongue, how could it avail to strengthen him on his
cold journey? These and other questions warn us against the
possibility of our own hubris blinding us to the interpretations of
this subtle novelist. It seems that the most fitting conclusion to
the polyvalent Golding is a series of interrogation marks.

MAUGHAM, LEWIS AND DE VRIES

Three Critics of the Church

The interest of our three novelists to be studied lies in the fact that they express profound criticisms of the institutional church by two writers outside and one writer inside that church. The first external criticism is that of Freud, in rather diluted form, as it appears in works by Somerset Maugham. Another criticism is that of Marx, as represented by the novels of the socialist Sinclair Lewis. The third form of criticism is internal and the work of one who is closely associated with the life of the present-day church, an accusation that Christ has been betrayed by the contemporary churches both by their cheapening of its message through a liberal accommodation to the world, and by reflecting instead of transforming the cultural and class divisions of the day.

Freud's criticism of the Christian church was most fully developed in *The Future of an Illusion*. Here Freud presents a modern variation of the argument, *timor fecit deos*, "fear created the gods." Man's fear of growing up, leaving the home, striking out on his own, grappling with the fierce competition of life, and the inevitable menace of death, Freud argues, created the image of a heavenly father who is alternately merciful and irate. This projected image provided security in time and safety beyond the grave, but at the same time it inevitably produced weak personalities who were unwilling to cut the knot that bound them to the womb. Like all religious persons, they were escapees from life, refugees from struggle, who lacked the courage to face the facts with courage. Moreover, the wish to placate this god led to a repression of human sexuality, which was always liable to break out again with fearful savagery, like the pent-up waters of a dam that bursts its retaining walls. Man is an orphan in the universe, says Freud, let him accept the fact that God is dead!

It is at least a partly Freudian and humanistic criticism of religion which emerges from the short stories and novels of Somerset Maugham. He implies in the short story "Rain" that the character Dr. Davidson becomes like the God he worships, that Dr. Davidson makes God in his own masterful and deceitful image. In a sentence, the story is that of a Calvinistic medical missionary who tries to run a prostitute out of his missionary territory only to commit adultery with her, and afterwards to shoot himself. Offended by the care-free happiness of the natives, unrestricted by his taboos, he determines to enslave them, first by stamping out dances, and then by forcing them to wear trousers. He is a caricature of the Calvinistic God in whom justice predominates over mercy. The victory that he is most proud of is his successful terrorizing of a Danish trader who was sexually and alcoholically indulgent, until he lost his business and came grovelling before Davidson. A sadist, Davidson worships a sadistic God. The man who is stern to others is indulgent to himself and his personal piety is a mess of saccharine sentimentality, an orgy of tear-streaming prayers. He begins by praying for, and ends by preying upon, Sadie Thompson, the prostitute, who has come to him in order that he may become the instrument of 'conversion.' The sardonic ending of the story comes with Sadie's outburst: "You men! You filthy dirty pigs! You're all the same, all of you. Pig! Pig!" The damned-up stream has broken its banks to become a sexual Niagara.

Now this story, "Rain," has a twofold interest. It has become the *stereotype* of the Christian as a repressed man or woman who is unfit for life and ultimately takes the logical step of suicide; this proves that human existence is based on an illusion and the illusion is directly traceable to religion. The significance of this in creating the Freudian stereotype was pointed out by Graham Greene in his book, *Journey Without Maps*. There he states that "Maugham has done more than anyone to stamp the idea of the repressed, prudish man of God on the popular imagination. "Rain" has impressed the image of Mr. Davidson over the missionary field." It might also be argued that his own novel, *The Power and the Glory*, was an attempt on Greene's part to rectify the stereotype, but that in making the priest the father of an illegitimate child, Greene did not overdo the propaganda! The other interest "Rain" holds is that it alerts us to the fact that the normally tolerant and even clinical objectivity of Somerset Maugham towards his characters is thrown out the window whenever he meets a Christian. This can be seen in his short story "The Verger," or in an early play, *The Loaves and Fishes*. It is strikingly evident in his most distinguished and autobiographical novel, *Of Human Bondage*.

The leading characters in the novel are the young adolescent Philip (Maugham himself, slightly disguised) and his uncle the Rev. Mr. Carey, the Vicar of Blackstable. The Vicar is for the author the official propagandist of that great illusion, Christianity; he is both deceiver and self-deceived. Repressed, he visits his displeasure on others, especially his wife. Though his nephew has a club-foot, he makes Philip take the long walk from the station to the vicarage instead of paying for a cab. The stove in the draughty hall is only lighted when the vicar himself has a cold. His exploitation of his curate is delightfully conveyed in a description of the hearthside equipment:

> Mr. Carey was making up the fire when Philip came in, and he pointed out to his nephew that there were two pokers. One was large and bright and polished and unused, and was called the Vicar; and the other which was much smaller and had evidently passed through many fires was called the curate.

A small cameo captures the miserliness and casuistical deceitfulness of the clergyman. When they are seating their small nephew at table, the maid produces a Bible and a prayer book to add to the chair's height. The naive Mrs. Carey is rather shocked by the treatment of these holy books and remonstrates: "Oh, William, he can't sit on the Bible." She begs the vicar to get some other books from the study. He considers the question for an

instant and replies: "I don't think it matters this once if you put
the prayerbook on the top, Mary Ann. The Book of Common
Prayer is the composition of men like ourselves. It has no claim to
divine authorship." The incident continues: "Philip perched himself on the books, and the Vicar, having said grace, cut off the top
from his egg. "There," he said, handing it to Philip, "you can eat
my top if you like." Philip would have liked an egg to himself, but
he was not offered one, so he took what he could . . . "How did
you like that top, Philip?" asked his uncle. "Very much, thank
you." "You shall have another one on Sunday afternoon." It
will have been observed that all Christians are, for Maugham,
divided into hypocritical knaves like the vicar and simple fools
like the vicar's wife.

Ultimately Mr. Carey's wife dies, and when his warden dis-
cusses the matter of a tombstone, suggests that a suitable inscrip-
tion would be, "With Christ, which is far better." But the vicar
opposes the suggestion, for he feels that it casts an aspersion on
himself. The final hypocrisy is that the Vicar, who so frequently
preaches the comfort of the Christian doctrine of the resurrection,
is himself terrifed by the prospect of death. He is willing to
preach this illusion to others, but he knows for himself that it is
still an illusion.

Is religion without value, then, in Maugham's eyes? Not
entirely—for it has a moral value if only it will rid itself of its
tiresome elements of miracle and mythology. One character in
the novel, Cronshaw the poet, says:

Perhaps Religion is the best school of morality. It is
like one of those drugs you gentlemen use in medicine
which carries another in solution: it is of no efficacy in
itself, but enables the other to be absorbed. You take
your morality because it is combined with Religion;
you lose the Religion and the Morality stays behind.

When all is said and done, the fact remains that the poet's view is one that Maugham's hero finds unconvincing. For only the slave accepts the "human bondage" of faith.

The second critique of the Church is the Marxist one. Like the Freudian, it claims that religion is an illusion, but it is also an ingenious modification of the same argument. The Marxist critique argues that the "haves," the Establishment, the capitalists, cunningly use religion in order to render the have-nots docile, for religion serves as the sanctification of the *status quo*. The Church compromises its original egalitarianism by accepting the hand-outs of the opulent, for whom it reserves the best seats, and whose costly memorials are displayed on its walls or in its stained-glass windows. The wars that Christianity hallows are recalled by the flags of the Lord of Hosts flanking its altars. Religion also serves a further function: it is the opiate of the masses. It promises a heavenly compensation for their earthly deprivations, a pie in the sky when you die. But the catch is—there is no heaven. So the only test of the value of a religion for the Marxist is whether it creates brotherhood; yet Christianity stratifies national and class divisions, despite its much-vaunted claims to fraternity. One recalls Archbishop William Temple's statement that "Karl Marx was the last of the Hebrew prophets," and that Communism had to be taken far more seriously than fascism because Christianity itself was the " most materialistic of religions."

In Sinclair Lewis we have, as his autobiography shows, less a Marxist then an old-fashioned and idealistic socialist. The figure of Christ has, for Lewis, a twofold importance. Christ was a preacher and martyr of the "brotherhood of men," and he also raised the dignity of artisans by his labors amid the sawdust and shavings, the chisel, saw, and hammer. For this reason Lewis chiefly directs his invective against the pervasive pietism of the era, which is a "glory to God and glory for me" kind of religion. While we may find the consistent hypocrisy of Lewis's novel *Elmer Gantry* (1927) too extreme to be convincing, we can also be impressed by some of the criticisms of the old-time pietistical religion and its orgies of emotionalism. Lewis gives a brilliant picture of mass-production evangelistic techniques in chapter fourteen, which owes not a little to his observation of Billy Sunday. The naked playing of the emotions, the suggestibility of the crowd, the faking of the statistics, the irrationality and unethical nature of these attempted conversions—all these practices are quite legitimately questioned.

Lewis returns to a religious theme in his novel *The God-Seeker* (1949). It is the story of the search for ideals by Aaron Gadd, a carpenter from the Berkshire hills of Massachusetts. Gadd is converted by a subordinate of the famous evangelist Charles Finney, and accepts an appointment at the hands of the American Board of Commissioners for Foreign Missions, under whose aegis he goes to be a missionary to the Indians. Gadd moves successively through the stages of Congregational Calvinism, Unitarianism, humanitarianism, until he finally achieves socialism—each stage is, of course, an advance in Lewis's view. Religious people in this novel are not deceivers of others, like Elmer Gantry; they are merely deluded themselves. And the most honest of them all, the protagonist, sees that what he always admired in the gospel of the carpenter of Nazareth was its socialistic overtones.

Lewis again unveils the mixed secular and spiritual motives in evangelicalism as he tells us about Aaron Gadd's conversion. The unctuous pietist who converts him appeals to Gadd first through the lure of adventure in the wild west, and then through Gadd's desire to convert the Sioux and gain glory in the world to come. There is a temptation to the free life, where he will be riding wild horses and not stuck forever in a New England village; he is tempted, too, by the thought of converting Indians who are perishing in their sins. Finally, the preacher baits the hook by promising that Gadd will get a free theological training and thus combine physical and spiritual adventures.

As for the mission itself, it is not an enormous success. Their most significant convert, Black Wolf, returns from Oberlin College

a convinced agnostic and highly critical of the missionaries'
naiveté. Lewis's view, I think we may claim from this novel, is
of Christianity as a benign illusion that fosters a morality of compassion and social reform. Where there is a minimum of super-
naturalism and theology, a maximum concern for social reform—
that is, Unitarianism—there you have the least harmful form of the
delusion. An honest man is the noblest work of God, says Lewis,
and honest men come out of the chrysalis of the outworn skin of
Christian superstition and fly their wings as free men dedicated to
the welfare of the community. The practical effect of a genuine
Christianity will, he argues, always be found in a regeneration of
the social order and through the expression of social justice. Here,
it seems to me, Lewis is worth listening to. For what else is the
God-Seeker but a sermon preached on the text: "How can a man
say that he loves his brother whom he has seen?" Such a faith,
genuinely color-blind and class-blind, would prove that Christianity has the authentic clue to human brotherhood and sister-
hood.

The third criticism of the Christian Church, and the wittiest, is
the wound of a friend. For Peter De Vries was brought up in the
Reformed Church of America, is an alumnus of Calvin College in
Michigan's Grand Rapids, and has served as a deacon in a Connec-
ticut Congregational Church. He is critical both of fundamentalism, because it is destructive of all reason, and of extreme
liberalism of the Unitarian variety because it destroys religious
commitment. His barbs are chiefly intended for the snobbishness
that turns a commuter's church into a club, instead of being a
local manifestation of the international and interracial church of
Christ. This critique is concentrated in his diverting novel, *The
Mackeral Plaza*, published in 1958; the character Mackerel is an
urbane and sophisticated clergyman.

In this novel De Vries objects to the smugness and self-
satisfaction of the street-corner evangelist who buttons an
ordained clergyman with the time-honored plea, "Brother, have

you found Christ?" The evangelist is discomfited by the unan-
swerable riposte of the clergyman, "What? Is he lost again?" In
a few lines De Vries tears to shreds revivalism as a mere religion of
incantation, drugging honest doubt with a sleeping-potion of
clichés: "Jesus is the power-house! Are you plugged in? Jesus
is the transformer! Are you wired up? Jesus is the cable carrying
that current from God Almighty! Is your trolley on?" But
De Vries uses a mere pea-shooter against fundamentalism, apparently convinced as he is of its sincerity. As I said, the high
explosive is directed to the liberal modernism that has compro-
mised the historic theology of the Church and therefore changed
it into a club for literary discussion, amateur dramatics, and affable
bohemianism.

In consequence the simplicities of the Christian imperatives to
take up one's cross and deny one's self, obeyed by fundamentalists, turn into complex compromises. Mackerel's sermon
concludes with the appeal: "Let us graft on to the Christian
principle of selflessness, as Auden so cogently urges, the Freudian
one of maturity, and come up with an ideal suited to our era."
This is simply a more complex way of saying, "God helps those
who help themselves." And it is stated in its simplest way as
"Help yourself."

Religion has been completely attenuated through conformity
to the culture. Religion, as the late Dr. Will Herberg was so fond
of pointing out, has been reduced in many parts of America to a
form of belonging; religion is narcissistic, the property of a culture
in love with itself and its smart up-to-dateness. Hence Mr. Mackerel wishes to be thought a layman; were he to be considered a
minister, set apart as God's witness, he would be quarantined from
the human race. There is a very revealing and amusing passage
describing a visit by Mackerel to the Zoning Board office in order
to complain about an orange and green advertising sign that reads
"Jesus Saves," which he claims is disturbing his meditations. The
well-upholstered secretary's reactions are as interesting as his:

'Oh, *you*'re the –?' She recoiled a step in surprise, then
laughed and said apologetically, 'But you're too young.
You can't be more than thirty-five. And you certainly
don't look like a preacher.'
Mackerel was delighted not to be thought too obviously
the conventional minister.

De Vries comments on his reaction:

Mackerel so disliked the term preacher, and so abhorred
the term brother, as designations for the clergy that he
was always grateful for their inapplicability to himself.
It was not merely the wish to elude prototype that lay
at the bottom of this, thought this wish did exist in
Mackerel to an exquisite degree; it was, more cardinally,
a fear of quarantine, a desire to belong to his species—
in which the deferential 'Reverend' tended to blur one's
membership—that made him want ever so much to be
known simply as Mister Mackerel.

Here De Vries is pointing out the pressures of intellectual and
social community that play upon any Christian. And it is all too
common a characteristic of suburbanite churches that they wish
to run with the hound of heaven and also hunt with the hares of
culture. This accommodation of the culture becomes clear in the
type of services that Mackerel conducts. His sermons show the
up-to-dateness of his reading so that he can retain his reputation
as the Hemingway of the pulpit, with his taut, ten-minute
sermons, punctuated with witticisms. When Miss Calico, a
woman friend and member of his congregation, questions him as
to his religious convictions, it is clear that Mackerel's beliefs are
vague and humanistic, somewhat idealistic, as were the man's who
defined the League of Nations as a vast cloud hanging over
Geneva. "I believe in belief," says Mackerel. "I believe that some
binding ethic, and some informing myth are necessary to any
culture, the myth being to the morality, what the wooden forms

are to the concrete poured into them. When the concrete is hard,
you remove the forms (or they will rot away) and the walls will
stand on their own." This is the exact counterpart of Somerset
Maugham's notion that morality is found in a soluble state in
religion; religion is the solvent. But the great difference is that
Maugham puts this view forward seriously, while De Vries is
satirical about it.

Ultimately, the ultra-liberal worship service is brilliantly shown
by De Vries to be no more than a service of community interdependence, and a pretty shallow one at that. This commuter's
community is blinded by self-love. They hold a service to which
every family is to bring a gift of food for the benefit of citizens
who were rendered homeless by flash-floods, and lay upon the
table under the pulpit a most unusual harvest festival: vichysoisse,
artichoke hearts, smoked clams, trout paté, and cocktail snacks
for flood victims. Entirely in keeping with this spirit, the incor-
rigible Mackerel prays: "Let us hope that a kind Providence will
put a speedy end to the acts of God under which we have been
laboring." In short, the ironic De Vries suggests that the hope of
Mackerel is, "Let God not be God."

What are the larger and more serious questions that De Vries is
asking of our modern neighborhood churches, behind his witty
raillery? Are these communities merely the cells of self-congratu-
lating ex-urbanites, and have they lost all sense of real unity and
mutuality in Christ, which transcends the divisions of race, class,
and culture? Are their ministers anything more than culture
vultures, amateur essayists and journalists, and psychologists, or
do they have an authentic revelation of the living God consum-
mated in the life, death and resurrection of Jesus Christ to
commend, which transforms society? Do these ten-minute dis-
quisitions on Havelock Ellis and Sigmund Freud, on self-expression and modern folkways, represent the mercy and judgment of
the Christian gospel, or are they merely opinions?

Here we have, the reply must surely be, a church not in
conflict with the world, but overwhelmed by it, not a gospel to

redeem the world here and hereafter through the crucifixion of the human ego, but merely good advice offered by the unregenerate to the unregenerate. This novel is, so it seems to me, the obituary of a religious liberalism bent on diluting doctrine, which exhausted itself by keeping up with the Einsteins and the Wittgensteins, and thus suffered acutely from snobbery. Its obituary is finely carved by H. Richard Niebuhr with the words, "A God without wrath brought men without sin into a kingdom without judgment through the ministrations of a Christ without a Cross." Such churches as De Vries depicts—and all our churches are tarred to some degree with the same brush—are fools for culture's sake, not fools for Christ's sake. Consequently they have never discovered, with St. Paul, that "the foolishness of God is wiser than men; and the weakness of God is stronger than men" (1 Cor. 1:25).

The criticisms of the Church that our three authors have borrowed from Freud, Marx, and others deserve fuller consideration than they were accorded in the novels just examined, because they are still widespread in contemporary life. One of the inestimable benefits that Sigmund Freud's researches have conveyed to the twentieth century is the knowledge that our human personalities are far more complex than we had previously supposed, and that the things we publicly abhor we may secretly admire. For Freud has revealed to us the mixed nature of our motives. He has shown clearer than ever before the deep and unconscious and powerful instinctual drives within us, which when satisfied give poise to our personalities and which when repressed and thwarted wreak vengeance on ourselves and our associates.

This knowledge can be wisely or unwisely used in our interpretation of religion and life. Unwisely used, Freud may become the justification for unbridled egotism and license; in the specious name of self-expression men have become satyrs in the guise of liberators, whom the Bible would have called adulterers, and women have become promiscuous in the guise of liberation whom the Bible would have called prostitutes. When this knowledge has

been wisely used, on the other hand, it has been of incalculable
benefit. In showing us how mixed all human motives are, and
how different our physical and psychic endowments as individuals
are, it has taught us to seek to understand others and to be less
censorious of them. Freud has freed us from such unnatural
concealment of sexual questions which are central issues of human
personality. He has given men and women greater equality in
marriage by indicating their deep sexual need of one another, and
helped explode the notion that the man is a savage and the woman
his unwilling victim.

One suspects that Freud was not able to do justice to Christianity for a very natural reason. As a brilliant and sensitive Jew in
Vienna, he was acutely aware of the bitter anti-Semitism of his
day and how his own people had been barred from their human
and social rights by the prejudice of Christians. The result is that
he repaid this anti-Semitism with anti-Christian polemic. It was
an eradicable and unconscious prejudice, but it serves as a warning
to both Gentiles and Christians.

The Marxist criticism of Christianity is one that is thorough-
going, and one we have to live with. There is no question that
the form of religion with which the Marxist revolutionaries were
most familiar—Russian Orthodoxy—had indeed become "the
opiate of the people." It was largely a form of social control in
the interest of the Czar and the aristocracy; it was muzzled and
bound and had no prophetic voice to use, like a modern Amos,
against those who were the exploiters. The words of Christopher
Caudwell, the Cambridge poet who died fighting for the international brigate in Spain, should not be forgotten. His literary
testament, entitled *Four Loyalties*, includes the condemnatory
words "I turned to Christianity, but I found most of them too
busy saving their own souls." On the Christian side, it is worth
recalling the words of the socialist Anglican bishop, Charles Gore,
who revealed his sense of the emptiness of charity in a laissez-
faire capitalist economy with the words, " 'Each for himself,' as
the elephant said when he danced among the chickens." The

turning of so many oppressed peoples recently liberated to communism should be a message to our Western democratic and religious tradition.

Without in any way sacrificing their Christian witness, indeed, by applying it, the Christian church should be in the forefront of the fight for social justice. The church should be proclaiming its individual and corporate gospel without fear or favor, and encouraging every technique that leads to the physical, moral, and spiritual benefit of the human race in all the varieties of natural, biological, and social science. Even so—by accepting so much of the truth of the Marxist critique—our Judeo-Christian heritage is bound to be severely critical of much in the theory and more in the contemporary practice of communism. We cannot condone the ruthless depersonalization of the individual, who cannot be reduced to the level of a unit of production and consumption, a cog in the gargantuan state machine. He or she is that brother or sister whom God created for everlasting fellowship with himself, that person for whom Christ died. In the second place, whoever has read Arthur Koestler's *Darkness at Noon*, the confession of a disillusioned lover of Communism, will oppose to their last breath the ruthlessness of the Communist methods of establishing the new society—the liquidation rather than conversion of its opponents, the brain-washing techniques. In the third place, we cannot accept the fantastic utopianism of communism—its assumption that the classless society will be paradise. In unredeemed human nature there is still the triple foe of utopianism: the corrupting egotism of power, the physical and mental suffering that is ever our dark companion in life, and the inexorability of death. To these three problems religion has the ultimate answer. Egotism is changed to God-regarding and neighbor-serving love. Suffering is accepted without bitterness by the Christian mystic as a participation in the sufferings of Christ. And Resurrection is the answer to the fear of death.

Finally we turn to the contemporary threat of liberal humanism, which De Vries emphasizes so vividly. His anti-hero,

Mackerel, is as the name suggests a very spotty fish of whom Jesus, the great fisherman, can hardly be proud. Mackerel's marching orders come not from the Christian gospel, but from the contemporary culture. That De Vries intends this is clear from the architectural plan of Mackerel's church, where the sanctuary occupies the smallest amount of space, and in the telegraphic brevity of his sermons, which proclaim the most recent gossip rather than the good news of the gospel. Mackerel's arrogance serves to distance him from the local fraternity of ministers, whose friendship, he believes, is not worth cultivating. Mackerel is an intellectual snob who confuses wit with wisdom. Who else would have thought he could add to the Beatitudes and deal with the problem of the danger to adolescent hot-rodders at the same time? The result was: "Blessed are the pacemakers, for they shall see God."

Here we see the ever-present danger of the cult of popularity, of teaching the latest message rather than the truth, of attempting to serve God with the methods of Mammon. De Vries knows from the inside the perils of confusing the suburban church with the City of God, and no one is his equal in puncturing inflated pride.

FLANNERY O'CONNOR

Anagogical Signals

Flannery O'Connor's stories shock her readers by their violence and horror, their grotesque characters, savage humor, and biting irony, not to mention their nightmare vision of evil she refuses to sentimentalize. Furthermore, the flood of books and pamphlets written to elucidate her work often makes the obscurity more obscure still. The present essay is written to provide an overview of her religious meaning by means of the clues she herself offers.

O'Connor uses the term "anagogical" to describe the deeper spiritual meaning contained in her short stories and novellas. The Greek word, *anagogē*, means an elevated sense, and, with reference to religious writings, a revelation of mystery. In time *anagogical,* as used in the adjectival form, came to be used to refer to the four levels of meaning in the medieval interpretation of the Scriptures. A fifth century work, John Cassian's *Conferences* (XVI, 8) distinguishes four levels of meaning: the literal; the allegorical, which applied any given passage to Christ and to the church militant; the tropological or moral, which applied the passage to the soul and its virtues; and the anagogical, which applied it to the heavenly realities. O'Connor seems to have used the term *anagogical* in a wider sense to refer both to the soul's relation to divine grace and to the soul's ultimate destiny, thus combining the tropological and anagogical levels in traditional Biblical exegesis.

Her understanding of the term as she reveals it in the posthumously published work, *Mystery and Manners*, is illuminating. There we find three separate references to its meaning. The first refers to the kind of creative vision that writers need to have as "anagogical vision, and that is the kind of vision that is able to see different levels of reality in one image or one situation."

Referring to medieval biblical interpretation, she called the
anagogical kind of meaning that "which had to do with the Divine
life and our participation in it." She insisted that this was an attitude
toward all of creation, and "a way of reading nature which
included most possibilities." In writing about her stories
O'Connor asked herself what it was that made her narrative work,
and concluded that it had to be "an action or gesture which was
both totally right and totally unexpected; it would have to be one
that was both in character and beyond character; it would have
to suggest both the world and eternity." The right action or
gesture is further described as one existing on the anagogical level,
"one that made contact with mystery." O'Connor's third reference to the anagogical approach is to the difficulty in our secular
culture in persuading readers to understand her fictional back-
woods prophets, who appear as grotesque freaks and perform
acts that can be described as "anagogical." A concern with grace,
she insists, is not concern for exalted human behavior. It is rather
"a concern with the human reaction to that which, instant by
instant, gives life to the soul. It is a concern with the realization
that breeds charity and with the charity that breeds action."
Clearly her stories, while believable on the narrative level, are
intended to be taken on the supernatural or anagogical level as
well.

O'Connor's deeper meaning is often difficult to gain, and for
a variety of reasons. It may be that the very grotesqueness of the
characters—for example Hulga, the woman with a Ph.D. and a
wooden leg who tries to seduce a Bible salesman—is the obstacle.
It could also be that our unfamiliarity with the *gesta Dei* as
revealed by the prophets of the Old and the apostles of the New
Testaments allows us to miss the clues to understanding that
Flannery O'Connor provides. We cannot, for example, understand the deepening hunger of the adolescent Tarwater in the
novella, *The Violent Bear It Away*, if we do not recognize
O'Connor's conviction that Christ is the bread of life that satisfies,
and that this satisfaction is conveyed in the Eucharist, of which
the miracle of the feeding of the five thousand with a few loaves

and fishes is the prototype and anticipation. It could also be that we confuse religion with ethics, and think of religious people as heroes who pull themselves up, Pelagian fashion, by their own bootstraps, instead of recognizing that it is those who know they are incomplete and sick who ask for healing and thus acknowledge the divine presence in grace and providence. But whatever the reason, Flannery O'Connor provides some significant anagogical signals, as I choose to call them, to illuminate her meaning, and the rest of this essay will go on to explore some of the more significant analogues she uses.

The first and most common theological pointer that O'Connor provides is *incompleteness*. Images suggesting lack of completeness point to the reality of original sin, the defect in the human being in need of grace for salvation. A physical defect, such as Hulga's wooden leg in "Good Country People," suggests she suffers from psychological twisting, too. The hearing aid of Rayber, young Tarwater's schoolmaster uncle in *The Violent Bear It Away*, implies that as a rationalist he is deaf to the divine call. The rationalists cannot hear the call of God, hence they need hearing aids. Immaturity can be amusingly conveyed by inappropriate shoes and curlers on an adult, as when Asbury's schoolteacher sister wears girl scout shoes in "The Enduring Chill" and "a white rag around her head with metal curlers sticking out from under the edges."

Another way of suggesting incompleteness is through images of atavism. It is surprising how frequently Flannery O'Connor likens her characters to animals, reptiles, or birds. In the novella *Wise Blood*, humans are described in animal terms no less than eight times. A boy has "a fox-shaped face," while a man on the street who is watching a potato-peeler salesman has the expression of "a grinning mandrill." Enoch Emery, a country boy trying to become an urban sophisticate, "looked like a friendly hound dog with light mange"; Slade, a sitter in a used car lot, has a face "under the cap like a thin pricked eagle's." Hazel Motes, the hero, who is haunted by Christ but wishes to wipe out his image,

preaches the Church without Christ. He happens to be a voyeur
and while he is watching a woman in the park pool, his face
becomes "sour and frog-like; it looked as if it had a shout closed
up in it." Motes preaches to a crowd as they are leaving a movie,
and the crowd includes a woman "with a cat-faced baby sprawled
over her shoulder." Hazel Mote's landlady, a schemer if ever there
was one, has "the disposition of a yellow-jacket and you could
hear her a block away, shouting and screaming at him." The most
striking animal image that occurs in *Wise Blood* is that of Enoch
Emery when he puts on a gorilla costume, which David Eggen-
schwiler aptly describes as "the instinctualist's apotheosis as an
ape." The very vividness of these zoological descriptions of
O'Connor's characters suggests that they who are allegedly made
in the image of God, are flawed, imperfect, requiring the com-
pleting work of grace.

O'Connor's method of describing human incompleteness is not
confined to one novella. It is interesting that such images also
occur in her second, *The Violent Bear It Away*. The welfare
woman who has come to take the adolescent hero away from his
great-uncle on the farm "bristled out of the corn, ruffled like a
peahen upset on the nest." And Tarwater's great-uncle, when
dead, is described as "a bull-like old man with a head set directly
into his shoulder and silver protruding eyes that looked like two
fish straining to get out of a net with red threads." When the
great-uncle takes Tarwater to the city to try to change his will,
the obdurate lawyer they consult, "a tall dome-headed man,
with an eagle's nose, kept repeating in a restrained shriek, 'But I
didn't make the law.' " Tarwater's great uncle, who considers
himself a prophet and whose sister schemes to commit him to an
asylum, realizes her intentions and rages "through her house like
a blinded bull, everything crashing behind him." When Tarwater's
schoolteacher uncle tries to give him an intelligence test, the boy
in his obstinacy is described as no more capable of being
"reasoned with than a jackal." The uncle, on learning from a
doctor of the probable future of his half-witted son, Bishop,
"saw himself facing the doctor, a man who made him think of a

bull, impassive, insensitive, his brain already on the next case."
Bishop clings to Tarwater at the edge of the lake, "like a large
crab to a twig." Finally, as Tarwater returns to the farm, he
stops at a wayside food stall, where the woman in charge insults
him. "He opened his mouth to overwhelm the woman and to his
horror what rushed from his lips, like the shriek of a bat, was an
obscenity he had once overheard at a fair."

It may be recalled that another Catholic writer, Graham
Greene, in *The Power and the Glory* as well as in other novels,
indicates the fallenness of the world by the seediness and decadence he ascribes to natural surroundings. For Flannery O'Connor,
however, the decadence is not found in nature, but in the grotesqueness of human nature and in its moral oddities. Whether
describing a brilliant sunset or the thousand whirling planets in a
peacock's tail, the natural splendor of the world is a reflection of
its Creator. While there is occasional ugliness in this created
world, more often it derives from our misuse of nature. For
example, when Tarwater reaches the city what he sees is "a hill
covered with used car-bodies. In the indistinct darkness, they
seemed to be drowning into the ground, to be about half-sub-
merged already." Another extreme example is found in the soiled
and curving streets of Atlanta in "The Artificial Nigger," which are
reminiscent of the circles of Dante's *Inferno* or the waterscape of
Camus' *The Fall*.

The moral incompleteness of human beings is also reflected in
the behavior of O'Connor's characters. Moral imperfection is seen
as a domineering figure in families, such as the son Asbury in "The
Enduring Chill" or in the figure of Grandfather Pitts, who
dominates his son-in-law and his granddaughter in "A View of the
Woods." The condescension shown by Mrs. Chestny in the title
story of the collection of short stories, *Everything That Rises Must
Converge*, very pleased with herself in offering a black child a
bright new penny, or by Mrs. Turpin who is surprised to find in
"Revelation" that blacks and white trash are in the company of
the saved, or by Mrs. May with her sense of superiority to white

trash in "Greenleaf," is also indicative of a moral failure. The
lack of supernatural charity is equally marked in the intellectual
snobbery of the Wellesley College girl who throws a book on
Human Development at Mrs. Turpin's head and then tries to
throttle her, in "Revelation," or in Asbury's arrogance toward the
faithful parish priest, and presumed equality with the Jesuit, in
"The Enduring Chill." Arrogant social workers, like Sheppard in
"The Lame Shall Enter First," who drives his own young son to
suicide, manifest in their overweening pride the reality of original
sin.

   Furthermore, the very language and idiom of O'Connor's
characters, which combine echoes of the English of the King
James Bible with the fractured English used by uneducated folk
in Georgia, also reflects a fractured world. Grandfather Pitts,
who is always affirming the superiority of his own family genes
to those of his son-in-law's family, is the one who misquotes the
Biblical adage which applies only too well to him: "Jedge not
lest ye be not jedged!" A choice example of this idiom is provided by a woman in the doctor's waiting-room in "Revelation,"
who informs the group where they can obtain a clock encased in a
sunburst of brass: "You can get you one with green stamps.
That's most likely where he got hisn. Save you up enough, you
can get you most anythang. I got me some joo'ry."

   Thus images of the grotesque, whether of outward appearance
or of behavior, all correspond to deficiencies of a moral kind and
point to the human need for salvation. This salvation does not lie
in education, for education can breed superiority and snobbishness. Similarly, the upward social mobility after which so many
of her characters strive is not a substitute for salvation, either;
least of all can the social sciences provide salvation, in O'Connor's
view, whose first degree was in social science. These are humanistic and false forms of salvation. For O'Connor, truth and grace
are found only in Christ. She was criticized even by pious Catholics for her striking preoccupation with the evil, the seedy, and the
violent, and defended herself by saying that although "good is the

ultimate reality, the ultimate reality has been weakened in human beings as a result of the Fall, and it is this weakened life we see." Moreover, to minimize evil is to underestimate the cost of restoration and redemption.

Another significant anagogical symbol in the stories of O'Connor is the use she makes of eyes and spectacles. Flannery O'Connor likes to insist upon the importance of careful observation of manners as the first requirement in a storyteller. But she also believed in the significance of vision, and quoted with approval Romano Guardini's observation that the roots of the eye are in the heart. The concentration on the eyes and the putting on or off of spectacles is a clue to new vision, or blindness of vision, in her stories. In "Everything That Rises Must Converge" Julian's mother has a seizure at the end of the story, and her face is gravely distorted as she lies dying: "One eye large and staring moved slightly to the left as if it had become unmoored. The other remained fixed on him, raked his face again, found nothing and closed." The unmoored eye sees eternity with a new and charitable gaze, and the death of his mother changes Julian because grace brings him to penitence, an "entry into the world of guilt and sorrow, for the pride that undervalued his mother." Similarly, in "A View of the Woods" Mary Fortune Pitts, the granddaughter, begs her violent grandfather to take off his spectacles and look reality in the face. But when she has been killed by the two blows of the rock he has banged against her head, and he hopes in his arrogance to see remorse on her face, we read; "He continued to stare at his conquered image until he perceived that it was absolutely silent, and there was no look of remorse on it. The eyes had rolled back down and were set in a fixed glare that did not take him in." Mary has another vision which, like Julian's mother, is no longer limited by human lenses.

The most significant use of this anagogical symbol is made in the novel, *Wise Blood*. One theme of this novel is the inability of Hazel Motes to resist Christ, whose prophet he has at last to become. In one scene a false prophet, Asa Hawks, pretends to be

blind. As a popular evangelist he has gathered a crowd together
because he has promised to blind himself, but he allows the lime
to cut his cheeks but never to enter his eyeballs. However the
true witness to Christ, Hazel Motes, blinds himself in reality in
order to see with the eyes of the soul. It is also important to
notice that Motes, in all his wanderings in the army and in his
career as anti-prophet and true prophet, keeps his Bible and his
silver spectacles, which belonged to his mother and which he
uses for reading the Bible. For his is the way of spiritual, not
corporeal, vision. Mrs. Flood, his landlady, asks hoarsely
whether one will be blind when dead, to which he replies that he
hopes so: "If there's no bottom in your eyes, they hold more."
Finally, the landlady stares at his empty eye-sockets, seeing them
as tunnels and Motes as "moving further and further into the
darkness until he was the pinpoint of light," Motes has become
a reflection of the Light of the World, an epiphany. The prayer
of the blind poet Milton is realized by Hazel Motes:

> So much the rather thou Celestial light
> Shine inward, and the mind through all her powers
> Irradiate . . . .

The strangest and most solemn of all O'Connor's anagogical
signals is the image of a sentinel line of black trees above a green
meadow with the red orb of the setting sun. This presence in the
sky is the moment of judgment and grace, and it occurs frequently
in her stories. Since her symbols are subtly polyvalent, the solar
disc which is bright white at midday, may also recall the continuing presence of Christ as the Host in the Mass.

For example, in the story "A View of the Woods," where the
trees seem drenched in blood, there is a veiled reference to the
Passion of Christ. When the grandfather, Mr. Fortune, gets up for
the third time to look at the woods, it is six o'clock and "the gaunt
trunks appeared to be raised in a pool of red light that gushed
from the almost hidden sun setting behind them." O'Connor continues, "The old man stared for some time, as if for a prolonged

instant he were caught up out of the rattle of everything and were held there in the midst of an uncomfortable mystery that he had not apprehended before." Then the image is made more explicit in its reference: "He saw it, in his hallucination, as if someone were wounded behind the woods and the trees were bathed in blood." He then returned to his bed and shut his eyes, and "against the closed lids hellish red trunks rose up in a black wood." Mr. Fortune is looking at the view of the woods he has sold, despite his children's and grandchildren's pleadings. The judgment against him is that his greed will not allow him to see the trees against the lake as beautiful, but only as "hellish red trunks."

The same image recurs powerfully in "Greenleaf." As Mrs. May dreams that she is walking over a series of rolling hills, she senses that the sun is trying to burn through the tree line. When she first stops walking, the sun "was a swollen red ball, but as she stood watching it began to narrow and pale until it looked like a bullet. Then suddenly it burst through the tree line and raced down the hill towards her." Later, as she walks through her own fields in reality, she reaches a green arena, encircled almost entirely by woods, while "through her closed eyes, she could feel the sun, red-hot overhead." Finally, a bull rushes at her, coming like a violent black streak over the horizon. In attacking her the bull has "buried his head in her lap, like a wild, tormented lover," with one of his horns piercing her heart, while the other curved round her side held her in an unbreakable grip. The story ends with these words: "She continued to stare right ahead, but the entire scene around her had changed—the tree line was a dark wound in the world that was nothing but sky—and she had the look of a person whose sight has been suddenly restored but who finds the light unbearable." Greenleaf, the hired man, shoots the bull four times in the eye and when he reached Mrs. May she seemed to be "bent over whispering some last discovery into the animal's ear." Here are several anagogical symbols: the blood-red tree line, the eyes, and the suggestion of a mystery unveiled. Blinding light suggests the eschatological revelation after death.

   The sun plays a leading role in *The Violent Bear It Away*,
when Francis Marion Tarwater comes to the lake to baptize
(and drown) Bishop. Its rays appear to provide a seal of approval
on what he is about to do: "The sun, which had been tacking
from cloud to cloud, emerged above the fountain. A blinding
brightness fell on the lion's tangled marble head and gilded the
stream of water rushing from his mouth. Then the light, falling
more gently, rested like a man on the child's white head. His
face might have been a mirror where the sun had stopped to
watch its reflection." The fountain is itself an image of baptism
and the child prepared for baptism is approved by the ray of
divine sunshine resting on Bishop's head.

   It is significant that O'Connor's other novel, *Wise Blood*,
when Hazel Motes leaves home in the train, he observes "the
train racing through tree tops that fell away at intervals and
showed the sun standing very red, on the edge of the furthest
woods," but for an ordinary person like Mrs. Wally Bee Hitch-
cock the sight was no more than the prettiest time of the day.
Some only observe; others, like Tarwater, have visions.

   The fourth anagogical signal is the significance of liturgical
colors and the revelatory events these colors symbolize. The
power of some liturgical colors may, of course, be due simply
to psychological association; it is natural to link red with blood,
white with purity, yellow with energy, purple with dignity,
gold with festivity, green with growth, light blue with hope,
and violet, dark blue and black with despair and mourning, and
the drabber earthy colors with burial. Current Roman Catholic
practice requires white for Easter, Christmas, and for feasts of
Christ, Mary, angels, and saints. Red is used for Passion and
Palm Sundays, Good Friday and Pentecost, and for feasts of
martyrs. Violet is used for Advent and Lent and occasionally
for funeral masses to replace black, while at most other times
green is used. A considerable use is made of violet or purple
by Flannery O'Connor; it is the color of preparation in the
seasons of Advent and Lent, and this color symbolism is typically

used early in a given story. In "Everything That Rises Must Converge" we find purple as a color in Mrs. Chestny's hat and observe the "dying violet of the sky" as Julian and his mother leave the house. In "A View of the Woods" Mr. Fortune is first seen sitting on his "mulberry-colored Cadillac," while Asbury Fox in "The Enduring Chill" drives with his mother and sister "staring out across a blurred purple-looking field," remembering another character, "Goetz, whose face had always been purple-splotched."

Purple has a more important premonitory significance, however, for it is sometimes mentioned immediately prior to the decision that brings grace or spiritual enlightenment in a story. In the short stories "Greenleaf," "Revelation," and "The Enduring Chill," the sky is purple at some crucial point in the story. In the first case "the sky was crossed . . . with purple bars," in the second, there is "a purple streak in the sky," and in the third the "sun moved serenely from under a purple cloud." In other stories, the color purple is woven into the fabric of the decisive act. The first time Mary Fortune deserts her grandfather and prepares for the alienation that will lead to her death at his hands, Mr. Fortune observes "a Negro boy drinking a purple drink." As Mrs. Turpin in "Revelation" thinks about her own humiliation and the unwelcome equalizing of social classes, "everything was taking on a mysterious hue . . . the streak of highway had turned lavender." This becomes the highway to heaven, on which the crowd is led by "whole companies of white trash" while Mrs. Turpin brings up the rear. In "Parker's Back" it is while Parker is hunting for a tattoo that will bring him peace in his own eyes, but actually emphasizes his hedonism, that he discovers a Christ with "sagging purple eyes."

The second color of great importance in Flannery O'Connor's stories is red, the liturgical color of Pentecost and the sign of the coming advent of the holy, purifying, and transforming Spirit, and of the martyrs, those whose witness to Christ is confirmed by their life's blood. Red is the color of the agency of grace in several of her stories. Mrs. Chestny is struck by a red pocketbook, which causes her eventually to take a much more humble view of herself. Mary Fortune shares her grandfather's red complexion, and the hogs of Mrs. Turpin's "Revelation" are suffused in a red glow. The combination of red and violence also appears in several of O'Connor's stories. In "A View of the Woods" the site of both the granddaughter's and her grandfather's death is on "an ugly red bald spot" on the ground; Asbury's moment of truth occurs in "The Enduring Chill" at the end of a red road. Even Mrs. May is gored by the bull under a "red-hot" sun. It should be observed, however, that there is a certain ambiguity in the color red as used in "A View of the Woods," where it may mean either that human sin is adding to the wounds of Christ, or that the glowing fires of hell consume the worshipper of Mammon forever.

The use of the color yellow is also ambiguous, since liturgically it may signify renewal, but on a natural level it may only be an indication of enlightenment. It may be important in "Revelation" that the sun's color changes with the progress of the story. It turns from blinding white to yellow and then to red, as Mrs. Turpin goes through various spiritual states. Beginning with blind ignorance as "the sun was getting whiter and whiter," she gradually reaches enlightenment ("the sun was a deep yellow" leading her to the hogs and humility), until at last the Holy Spirit and grace break over her at the pig pen, where "the sun was . . . very red." In "Everything That Rises Must Converge" a brilliant sunrise is used as a metaphor for enlightened vision. Asbury rides with his relations "on a road stretched between two open fields of yellow bitterweed" suggesting the bitter enlightenment through which he must proceed, through the later purple field before he finally goes along the red road of the Spirit in a room with a faded blue rug of past innocence for his chilling experience of grace. Yellow appears twice in "Parker's Back" and both examples of its use are striking; in each instance, O.E. Parker is about to learn something of importance. In the first place, when "two or three yellow streaks crossed the sky," Parker is forced to admit his two prophetic Christian names which he has previously hidden in the initials O.E., and is forced to confront himself. Second, "a yellow glow" envelops Parker and his wife as he realizes that his tattoo is regarded as mere idolatry by his wife, and that it is the Holy Spirit, not a name or a picture, who controls human destiny.

The color of gold, red and yellow, also has a special signifi- cance for O'Connor in *The Violent Bear It Away*. It is the color of the divine fire that purifies humanity, the color of the burning bush which was not consumed as Moses saw it and put off his shoes in reverence before it, and the color of the fiery furnace in which Daniel as God's faithful servant was preserved. When Tarwater, having fulfilled his commission to baptize Bishop, returns to his home, he sees the divine presence which will com- mission him to "GO WARN THE CHILDREN OF GOD OF THE TERRIBLE SPEED OF MERCY." "There, rising and spreading in the night, a red-gold tree of fire ascended as if it would con- sume the darkness in one tremendous burst of flame. The boy's breath went out to meet it. He knew that this was the fire that had encircled Daniel, that had raised Elijah from the earth, that had spoken to Moses and would in the instant speak to him." Tarwater throws himself to the ground in an act of abasement and reverence.

There is a final anagogical signal in O'Connor's fiction deserving consideration, and this is the clue she offers when she uses the device of a simile, preceded by the phrase "as if," a device she later gave up on the advice of the writer Caroline Gordon. The phrase is often followed by important theological terms. Thus we are given a clue to the inner meaning of the story of "Everything That Rises Must Converge" when we are informed that Julian "walked along, saturated in depression, as if in the midst of his martyrdom he had lost his faith." His pride makes him a false martyr, or he would not think himself superior to the mother who has worked herself to the bone for him. Like so many of the young adults in her fiction, he stands convicted of ingratitude and arrogance. His condemnation is indicated by the information that Julian sits beside a black man "as if it were for his mother's sins." He thinks he is making atonement for his mother's sins, but in fact he is committing the further sin of retaliation.

In "The Lame Shall Enter First," the fact of original sin is indicated by the phrase "as if Rufus Jones had some elementary warping of nature." In both "Greenleaf" and "Revelation" a crucial point in the story is reached with the signal "as if waiting for a revelation." The same is true in "A View of the Woods": the phrase "as if" is used when the grandfather who is making the entire family with whom he lives unhappy by selling off the best view from their house, suddenly gets a chance for reconsideration and repentance.

An indication that grace ultimately cannot be resisted is provided in "Parker's Back," when "a calm descended on the pool hall as if the long barn-like room were the ship from which Jonah had been cast into the sea."

The following passage from *The Violent Bear It Away* unites three striking symbols by this syntactical device. At the moment that Tarwater is about to baptize Bishop, "part of a red globe hung almost motionless in the far side of the lake as if it were the other end of the elongated sun cut through the middle by a swatch of forest." The stationary red globe is a reminder of the sun standing still for Joshua, the red liturgical color also points to the advent of Christ and the Spirit, and symbolizes the continuing presence of Christ in the communion Host. Shortly afterward we read another sentence which emphasizes the coming of grace with the premonitory color of purple combined with the expected formula: "The sky was an intense purple as if it were about to explode in darkness."

There is subtlety and profundity in Flannery O'Connor's fiction. Yet the obscurity in the anagogical interpretation of her stories will be reduced considerably for those acquainted with the Bible and the catechetical tradition of the Roman Catholic

church. Her stories are, in fact, parables well worth probing both
for their religious insights and their brilliant observation of
humanity. Again and again Flannery O'Connor insists that her
task is to observe the manners of people with vivid exactitude, but
also with the vision of mystery that Catholicism provides for
understanding life. Her editors, Sally and Robert Fitzgerald,
rightly called her explanatory lectures on her craft as a writer
Mystery and Manners. My concern has been to note the forms
she uses to express the supernatural mystery which she terms
'anagogical' in its range and depth. Her briefest definition of her
subject as author is the following: "I have found, in short, from
reading my own writing, that my subject in fiction is the action of
grace in territory held largely by the devil." That is why we find
in her stories grotesqueness, violence, and supremely, mystery.

FREDERICK BUECHNER

The Paradox of Grace

Religious novelists are in short supply in a secular century.
François Mauriac, despite his preoccupation with the struggle of
Christ in his characters for dominance over the counterclaims of
money and love, was a convinced Catholic novelist, who won the
Nobel Prize. Another Catholic novelist, Graham Greene, has yet
to gain that coveted award, despite the fact that he has been
nominated year after year with monotonous regularity. Frederick
Buechner is that rarer bird, a Protestant novelist, and, more exotic
still, an ordained Presbyterian minister who has never been in
charge of a parish or taught a theological seminar. He modestly
terms himself "part-time Christian and part-time novelist." In
fact, he is much more: both a brilliant novelist and an imaginative apologist for the Christian faith, as can be seen most convinc-
ingly in his Bebb tetralogy, and in his theological writings,
particularly the Lyman Beecher lectures at Yale entitled *Telling
the Truth, the Gospel as Tragedy, Comedy, and Fairy Tale*
(1977).

It is a matter of the greatest interest that Buechner has always
considered the writing of his novels as an exercise of ministry.
His justification for leaving Phillips Exeter Academy after ten
years—first as chairman of the department of religious studies
and later as school minister—to become a full-time freelance
writer was precisely to use a writer's wider pulpit. In an interview
printed in *Publishers' Weekly* in 1971, Buechner claimed that

> writing *is* a kind of ministry. I do not feel I am doing
> much different in my preaching and in my writing.
> Both are designed to illuminate what life is all about,
> to get people to stop and listen a little to the mystery of
> their own lives. The process of telling a story is some-

thing like a religion if only in the sense of having a plot
leading to a conclusion that makes some kind of sense.

For such concentration he has had to pay a price. As he informed
me in a frank interview in his home in southern Vermont in
August of 1981, the world of literature is offended by his persis-
tent theological obsession, and the more conventionally religious
are unable to understand his use of off-beat characters and his
uncensored colloquial language. Buechner is too religious for the
sophisticated, but not religious enough for the conservative and
conventional. That is, come to think of it, the perfect place for an
innovative and imaginative apologist is to be standing, between the
unbelievers and the believers.

It is important to stress the profound understanding Buechner
demonstrates in all his writings for the skeptic, and for the
cogency of the skeptic's viewpoint. Buechner is able to do this
because he was in that position himself for many years. This is
one advantage he has in not being brought up in any religious tradition and, therefore, in having to fight for the faith. As Nancy B.
Myers reminds us in her admirable doctoral dissertation for North
Texas University entitled, *Sanctifying the Profane: Religious
Themes in the Fiction of Frederick Buechner* (1976), Buechner
found great comfort in Paul Tillich's statement that doubt is not
the opposite of faith, but an integral part of faith. That he did so
is shown in two ways in Buechner's novels.

First, there is always a character who serves as a devil's advocate, whose cynicism is a foil to any tendency there might be to
adopt a mindless optimism that ignores sin, suffering, and death.
Secondly, the characters who are motivated by religion are also
subject to the ambiguities of human existence. The result is that
they are not cardboard creations, but human beings wavering
between faith and doubt as the forces of evil and the pressures of
materialism assail them. His remarkable collection of skeptics
and cynics include the honest patrician of a politician, Ansel Gibbs
(in *The Return of Ansel Gibbs*, 1958), who is world-weary, and

the malicious gossip of a local journalist, Will Poteat, in a fine autobiographical novel about the life of a New England minister called *The Final Beast* (1965). In the Bebb tetralogy the role of the skeptic is played by the ex-Catholic writer Antonio Parr, who sets out determined to expose Bebb, the phony evangelist running a correspondence diploma mill that creates ministers at five dollars per contribution, and who ends by finding that Bebb is more honest than he. Also, it is Bebb himself who, although he says he believes everything, also insists that it is "hard as hell."

Never for a moment does Buechner abandon the idea that to have and keep faith is difficult in our profane culture. He returns to his central theme again and again. An early novel, *The Season's Difference* (1952), is wholly concerned with the possibility of convincing others of a mystical vision. Peter Cowley informs the visitors to a summer colony that he has had a vision from God, and desires to take all the adults to the place in the hope that all will see the vision. His plan does not include the children, but they on their own are determined to be included, and they dress in white sheets and enact a "vision" which deceives the adults for a few minutes. Then Buechner is able to provide us with a panorama of different reactions to the supernatural, varying from total disbelief to credulity. By implication, therefore, Buechner had already envisaged all the problems involved in being a Christian apologist, even before he was ordained. Cowley's solution in this novel is the recognition that positive proofs of God's existence, such as miracles or visions, are no longer necessary and that belief itself is miraculous enough; we should not demand that God produce an identity card. In *The Alphabet of Grace* (1970), Buechner makes this point more explicitly. "Perhaps it is my believing itself that is the miracle I believe by." If God could be revealed in a manner that would expel all doubt, then there would be no room either for faith or for the exercise of freedom in the individual.

The search for faith is a theme that persists in Buechner's novels. In *The Final Beast*, the minister Nicolet feels as though some certitude which has previously escaped him is shortly to be vouchsafed. So he goes to an opening in the woods and lies flat on his back, with his arms stretched out, and whispers "Please" to God. Does anything happen? Nothing demonstrable, yet Nicolet's outlook is changed. It was the result of "the occasional, obscure, glimmering glimpse of grace." The "muffled presence of the holy" is what Buechner calls such moments in *The Alphabet of Grace*, where he goes on to define it as "images, always broken, partial, ambiguous of Christ." All that the outer ear could hear was the click-clack of the branches rubbing against each other, yet they were offering their own *benedicite* in praise of God. Faith, as Buechner suggests in *The Final Beast*, is a dance to the tunes of unheard music—a joy at the heart of the universe. The novelist has always associated faith and the capacity to receive grace with innocence. So adults in his novels have an acute need to become his children, to shed sophistication, for "as a child you took the language of faith literally, then you learned to take it symbolically, before you could see you had been more right in the first place."

Faith, says Buechner in his *Wishful Thinking: A Theological ABC* (1973), is "on-again-off-again rather than once and for all . . ." It is surely significant that the character who shows the most serenity in all of Buechner's fiction, the minister Nicolet, reaches this calm assurance after losing his wife and bringing up his two daughters as a widower, helped by a German refugee woman who had been brutally treated in a concentration camp. He lives to see her burnt body brought out from the manse which has been set on fire by two malevolent youths. This is the woman of whom Buechner writes, "God made Irma Rheinwasser very angry. He asked so much of his servants and rendered so little . . . 'If you got God for a friend you don't need any enemies.' " Buechner has no cotton wool in his ears to prevent him from hearing the cries and curses of humanity, nor does he wear rose-colored glasses to hide from the sight of its festering wounds. Faith is always a fighting faith. That is why his novels are so bracing to read.

If the difficulty of overcoming reason and skepticism by faith
is one primary concern of Buechner's, another is his interpretation
of sin. It seems as though Buechner has two complementary ideas
about sin. Whereas we might expect his interpretation of sin to
take the orthodox theological forms of transgression or trespass
against God's holy laws, or, more profoundly, as rebellion against
God, neither concept appears to be used by Buechner. The reason
for this must surely be that the sophisticated worldlings who are
his readers find it impossible, or only barely possible, to believe
in God. They cannot be thought of as either rebelling against God
or against a divine code. Hence humanists must conceive of sin,
as a start, as either a phenomenon that leads to separation from
each other (rather than separation from God) or as sheer waste of
personality.

The primary sense in which sin is depicted in Buechner's
earlier novels is that of alienation from other people. The more
egotistical a character becomes, the less his acquaintances can
trust him, and so the more he becomes an isolate needing the
forgiveness of others to rejoin the human race. Incidentally, *The
Final Beast* is a remarkable parable on the theme of forgiveness,
for the act of forgiveness involves all the characters of the novel,
including even Irma Rheinwasser. Her victimization at the hands
of a Nazi prison director, who tore out some of her toes to make
her feet look like the awkward chicken he said the rest of her
body resembled, made the act of foregiveness on her part almost
a miracle.

One image that Buechner uses for sin as a tragic waste is drawn
from the evil custom in Florida of dumping truckloads of peaches
to rot on the side of the road, in order to create a relative shortage
and thus force up the price. This induced rottenness is a fitting
symbol of the incompleteness of so many lives.

One of the great difficulties Buechner admits he faces is his
inability to create a truly evil character. He began to create such a
person in the cynical, hard-nosed and malicious Will Poteat in

The Final Beast, but while Will Poteat never becomes a lovable character, we do begin to feel sympathy for him toward the end of the novel. This incapacity to create a credible and consistently evil character is a consequence of Buechner's remarkable charity.

A third relevant topic that intrigues our novelist is that of discovering whether life has any meaning, plot, or pattern. So many of our contemporaries, as Camus documented in *The Fall*, find themselves overwhelmed by ennui if they are well-to-do, or by the sheer mechanical repetitiveness of their jobs and of their pleasures if they are not. One of the major lures of Christianity for Buechner is that it gives purpose to human existence. This theme dominates his extremely interesting Lyman Beecher lectures on preaching, which must be the most vivid and superbly illustrated of the entire series. No wonder Buechner wondered for a while, like John Updike, whether he should become an artist in color rather than in words. Here, with extraordinary insight, he shows that the gospel has three phases. He begins with what Chesterton called the good news of original sin, but Buechner does not call it that. Rather, he insists that in this fallen world tragedy is inevitable, and that the honest person will recognize it; indeed, he rejects the bland optimism of a character called Kitten Dory in *The Return of Ansel Gibbs*, who denied that Jesus ever died, with the ringing words: "If this Jesus of hers didn't suffer like everybody else, then he was never really one of us, and Christianity's based on a masquerade."

But the second point Buechner makes in the Beecher lectures is the place of comedy in this universal and inevitable tragedy that is life. Comedy is unpredictable, free, hilarious, like God's grace. Abraham's wife Sarah has a child when she is long past the childbearing age, which Buechner describes as hilarious and unpredictable. It is the God of surprises who "put his finger on Jacob the trickster, Noah who hit the bottle," Moses "who was trying to beat the rap in Midian for braining a man in Egypt, or the prophets who were mad as hatters." Typical of the divine upsetting of human norms and assumptions that Buechner marvellously chronicles in the Bible, and also typical of his own irony, is the following passage:

> The tragic is the inevitable, the comic is the unforseeable. Who could have foretold that out of the sordid affair between David and Uriah's wife Bathsheba, Solomon would be born with his high IQ and his passion for ecclesiastical architecture and that out of Solomon would be born a whole line of apostate kings ending finally in a king the likes of whom nobody could possibly have foretold, except maybe the second Isaiah, who saw at least that it wasn't his *beaux yeux* that would draw men to him nor by the power of heavy artillery that he would be king it over them?

It is not, of course, the first time that Christianity has been interpreted as a tragi-comedy; the move from the crucifixion to the resurrection of Christ makes this the inevitable dramatic gesture in which to conceive the gospel. The originality of Buechner's interpretation is to be found in the third category he uses, that of myth, although he still insists on the gospel's historical validity. He draws four parallels between the gospel and a fairy tale: it is a world of darkness, danger, and ambiguity; the real perils are all the more perilous because they are not realized as such; nothing is apt to be what it seems, which is also true of the identity of the hero; both fairy tales and gospel stories are "tales of transformation where the ones who live happily ever after, as by no means everyone does in fairy tales, are transformed into what they had it in them at their best to be."

So the world revealed in the gospel helps us to penetrate the incognito of the humble Christ, for in the striking words of Buechner, "And the king, unshaven, and clothes picked from a rummage sale, split lip, pants that didn't fit, and a black joke written in three languages over his head on the cross. But the whole point of the fairy tale is that he is king despite everything." Similarly, in the world of the gospel the people who consider

themselves righteous are seen to be fakes, and it is the ones who
are the dregs of society who drink the cup of salvation as Christ
offers it. Again let Buechner's incisive words etch the contrast.
"In the world of the gospel it is the killjoys, the phonies, the nit-
pickers, the holier-than-thous, the loveless, cheerless, and irrele-
vant who wear the fancy clothes and go riding around in sleek
little European jobs marked Pharisee, Corps Diplomatique,
Clergy." Who are their opposites? The potentially good "go
around like the town whore, the village drunk, the crook from
the IRS, because that is what they are—they stand a chance of
being saved by God because they don't stand a chance of being
saved by anyone else!" The marvelous reality is that this fairy
tale is true, and that it did not only happen once upon a time
but has kept on happening ever since and goes on happening
still.

   With such insights into God's hilarious transvaluations and
amazing choices, and the completely unforeseeable and unpredictable character of God's grace, we are prepared for Buechner
to take this biblical vision with a shattering seriousness in his
Bebb tetralogy. No set of novels in contemporary culture better
deserves the title of "God's strange work." These four novels
display a theological profundity and fidelity to the biblical revelation, a christocentric compassion for all types and conditions of
his characters, and a cleansing of humor that also punctures pride
and pretentiousness, making him a foremost interpreter of God's
strange ways in contemporary culture.

   As I hinted earlier, the choice of characters and events to
demonstrate the working of divine grace and the earthy language
used by the unredeemed or partly redeemed may very well shock
conventional readers. But only thus can Buechner point out that
God does not have heroes. For heroes succeed by means of their
own strength, but only those in the process of becoming saints
have lives which illustrate what St. Paul meant when he said, "We
have the treasure in earthen vessels that the power may be seen to
be God's." I think that even after this preliminary warning many

new readers may be offended by Buechner, but others will be
attracted by his saltiness.

The most fully rounded character Buechner has created in
his novels is Leo Bebb, who—taking the Protestant principle of the
priesthood of all believers literally—is ready to give anyone a
diploma of ordination to the ministry on payment of a five dollar
fee. This character, introduced in *Lion Country* (1971) as an
oddity, is the nearest character to a saint in the four novels. His
reflection of the generosity of God is glimpsed partly in his affection for Lucille, his Tropicana-spiked-with-gin drinking wife with
the dark glasses; the gin and the glasses both indicating that she
has done everything possible to escape from the horror of remembering that in a drunken stupor she killed their only child, the
joy of Leo's life. His life is one unqualified act of forgiveness
without condescension. His is a faith to move mountains. Indeed,
we are led to believe that it was strong enough to bring his homo-
sexual assistant, Brownie, back from death by electrocution.

But Leo Bebb, who is not afraid to leave his car in a Florida
reproduction of a safari in the Sahara and face lions like an early
Christian, was once jailed for exposing himself. Moreover, the
power of this temptation has not entirely lost its force. In a
climactic scene Bebb is approached by Redpath, a millionaire
Red Indian chief, and father of his people in more than a meta-
phorical sense, to pray for the restoration of his sexual powers
in the Church of Holy Love, Inc. As the scene unfolds Bebb
prays in the packed church, drawing upon Psalm 103:5, in scarce-
ly veiled *double entendres*. But at this moment, Bebb's pulpit
gown billows out, once more exposing him in public. We are left
in the dark as to whether this act of exposure was unintended or
deliberate on Bebb's part, but the scene is a good example of
Buechner's awareness of the ambiguities of the human condition.

If we look for the quality of grace in Bebb, we would find it
dramatically displayed in *Love Feast*, the third novel of the series,
where Bebb goes out into the "highways and byways" of

Princeton and collects all the unhappy students and citizens in
Alexander Hall for the convivial feast of the Great Supper
envisaged in Luke's gospel. His chief antagonist in this novel is an
atheist, instructor Virgil Roebuck of the history department, who
has a crippled son, and who uses his authority to stop these love-
feasts. Bebb visits Roebuck in his university office, and they
battle out their respective views of God. But, as Bebb later told
his son-in-law Parr, he could not help seeing this man with compassion. He saw the name "Virgil" printed on a deskplate and
realized his parents had expected Virgil Roebuck to become a
great scholar, and he wasn't, and wouldn't ever be. Bebb also
saw behind his criticism of God the fact that he had been given a
crippled son who couldn't, by himself, even manage the routine
business of urinating. Then Bebb, with a profoundly Christian
charity observed: "Antonio, I butted in there mad as a hornet,
but you can't stay mad when you start thinking things like that.
Once you commence noticing the lines a man's got around his
eyes and mouth and think about the hopeful way his folks gave
a special name to him when he was first born in this world, you
might as well give up . . . I said, 'The night is dark, Virgil Roebuck,
and home's a long way off for both of us.' " One recalls Graham
Greene's profound comment in *The Power and the Glory*, that
hatred is a failure of the imagination. Compassion is brought to
a fine sensitivity in Buechner's novels. He enables us, among
other Christian insights, to recognize the image of God beneath
the filth and the recriminations, the foulness and the failures.
He enables us to recognize the image of God behind the unlike-
liest of human exteriors.

In a book of sermons preached when he was a school chaplain, *The Magnificent Defeat* (1968), Buechner sums it all up:

There are moments when we are sure that everything
does make sense because everything is in the hands of God,
one of whose names is forgiveness, another is love . . . .
Jesus was the love of God alone among us, and not all the
cruelty and blindness of men could kill him . . . This is our

glory and our only hope. And the sound that it makes
is the sound of excitement and gladness and laughter that
floats through the night air from a great banquet.

All Protestantism in general, and American Presbyterians in particular, can rejoice that in their midst is a man and a novelist who
has found his calling as a minister of the Word of God to culture.
But like most faithful ministers he deserves a wider congregation
of believers and unbelievers to whom to proclaim the strange and
searching ways of the grace of God, which only a humble and
empty hand can accept, and by means of which the ordinary
person becomes extraordinary.

SOURCES

1   "I have heard . . . . king." *Hamlet* 2.2.

5   "The tension . . . litterateur." Marie-Helene Davies, *Laughter in a Genevan Gown: The Works of Frederick Buechner: 1970-1980* (Grand Rapids, MI: Eerdmans, 1983), p. 136.

       "easier . . . Bank." *Peculiar Treasures* (New York: Harper & Row, 1979), preface.

7   "O . . . notion." Robert Burns, "To A Louse."

GERARD MANLEY HOPKINS

13   "is not a society . . . sanctities . . . constitutions require." Chester Burns, SJ, "Gerard Manley Hopkins, Poet of Ascetic and Aesthetic Conflict" in *Immortal Diamond: Studies in Gerard Manley Hopkins,* (New York: Sheed and Ward, 1949), pp. 174-91.

16   "Be thou, then . . . fold thy child." References to the poems are from *The Poems of Gerard Manley Hopkins*, ed. W. H. Gardner (London and New York: Oxford University Press, 1942).

18   "God's utterance. . . . to name and praise him." Unpublished ms. cited in John Pick, *Gerard Manley Hopkins, Priest and Poet* (London: Oxford University Press, 1942), p. 49.

19   "The busy working . . . . beauty comes home." *Journal*, 25 August 1870; 17 August 1878.

22   "I always knew. . . . I will not." Hopkins to Bridges, 18 October 1882.

D.H. LAWRENCE

25   "pornography. . . . unpardonable." "Pornography and Obscenity," *The Portable D.H. Lawrence* (New York: The Viking Press, 1947), p. 653.

28   "My great. . . . bridle." D.H. Lawrence to Ernest Collings, 17 January 1913.

29   "The Catholic . . . magnificent God." *Phoenix: The Posthumous Papers of D.H. Lawrence* (New York: The Viking Press, 1936), p. 396.

30   "Heaven. . . . worth hiding." *The Rainbow* (New York: The Viking Press, 1961), p. 2.

"To know. . . . being." *Studies in Classic American Literature* (New York: Penguin Books, 1977), pp. 101-2.

31   "See, you. . . . two souls." *Sons and Lovers* (New York: The Viking Press, 1913), p. 251.

"I asked. . . . bodies." *The Man Who Died* (London: Martin Secker, 1931), p. 137.

32   "Can I not . . . earth's humus?" *Rainbow*, pp. 264-5.

"It's a sort . . . earth." *Women In Love* (London: Martin Secker, 1921), p. 134.

33   "I often. . . . artist." *Collected Letters* (New York: The Viking Press, 1962), p. 189.

34   "Never . . . sex." E. and A. Brewster, *Reminiscences and Correspondence of D.H. Lawrence* (London: Martin Secker, 1934), p. 122.

"God forbid. . . . sort." D.H. Lawrence to Lady Ottoline Morrell, 28 December 1928.

"the act . . . novel." Mark Spilka, *The Love Ethic of D.H. Lawrence* (Bloomington, IN: University of Indiana Press, 1955), p. 178.

37   "dead protoplasm." *Studies*, p. 102.

"So the children . . . life." *Rainbow*, p. 279.

38   "live and . . . analysis." "Hymns in a Man's Life," *Assorted Articles* (London: Martin Secker, 1932), pp. 157-60.

CHARLES WILLIAMS

41   "preoccupation . . . maturity." F.R. Leavis, *The Common Pursuit* (London: Chatto & Windus, 1952), p. 252.

"They seem . . . century." C.S. Lewis, introduction to *Essays Presented to Charles Williams* (London: Oxford University Press, 1947).

42   "in his company . . . some principle . . . another." Mary McDermott
      Shideler, *Charles Williams* (Grand Rapids, MI: William B. Eerdmans,
      1966), p. 6.

45   "a thing. . . . relish it." *Shadows of Ecstasy* (London: Gollancz,
      1933), pp. 36-7.

47   "safeguarding . . . citizens." Mary McDermott Shideler, *The Theology
      of Romantic Love* (New York: Harper and Brothers, 1962), p. 64.

      "In the last. . . . whole." "What the Cross Means to Me," in *What the
      Cross Means to Me* (London: James Clarke and Co., 1943), p. 147.

49   "If you. . . . universe." *Descent Into Hell* (New York: Pellegrin,
      1947), p. 106.

52   "refused. . . . himself gain." *All Hallows Eve* (London: Faber &
      Faber, 1945), p. 178.

53   "There around her. . . . soul." *Eve,* pp. 188-9.

55   "Since. . . . of the City." *Eve*, pp. 270-1.

                              C.S. LEWIS

59   "The moral. . . . degree." *English Literature in the Sixteenth Century*
      (London: Oxford University Press, 1954), p. 42.

60   "In the Trinity. . . . liberation." *Surprised by Joy* (New York:
      Harcourt, Brace, 1956), p. 215.

61   "All things. . . . but not out." *The Pilgrim's Regress* (New York:
      Sheed and Ward, 1935), p. 143.

      "You mean . . . all." *Pilgrim's Regress*, pp. 147-8.

63   "The fox . . . itself." *Joy*, p. 212.

64   "Such then . . . military service." *Joy*, p. 164.

      "But though . . . Zoo . . . the organ least." *Joy*, pp. 220-1.

ALBERT CAMUS

67   "getting up. . . . set in." *The Plague* (New York: The Modern Library, 1948), p. 4.

68   "No morality . . . condition." *The Plague*, pp. 5, 75.

70   "I leave. . . . happy." *The Myth of Sisyphus and Other Essays* (New York: Knopf, 1955).

73   "it was wielded . . . floor." *The Plague,* p. 87.

74   "I understand. . . . grace.' " *The Plague*, p. 197.

75   "The sufferings . . . to compass." *The Plague*, pp. 201, 203.

76   "Why . . . silence?" *The Plague*, p. 118.

    "For. . . . my peace." *The Plague*, p. 228.

78   "The Greeks. . . . attitude." Jean Onimus, *Albert Camus and Christianity* (University, AL: University of Alabama Press, 1970), p. 37.

    "For . . . of revolt." Onimus, p. 34.

GREENE AND MAURIAC

83   "the unbaying . . . hunter." *A Woman of the Pharisees*, trans. Gerard Hopkins (London: Eyre and Spottiswoode, 1946), p. 208.

85   "Saints . . . imagination." *The Power and the Glory* (New York: The Viking Press, 1940), p. 139.

    "You must. . . . world." *Pharisees*, p. 107.

86   "One can. . . . No." *Pharisees*, p. 142.

    "I now stand. . . . own merits." *Pharisees,* pp. 177-8.

88   "Each one. . . . his choice." *Pharisees,* p. 185.

87   "I'm not interested. . . . like himself." *The Power*, pp. 232-3.

90   "In the evening. . . . our love." *Pharisees*, p. 203.

92   "(Pinkie) 'I don't take . . . I don't,' he said." *Brighton Rock* (New York: The Viking Press, 1951), p. 128.

93   "The power. . . . We feel. . . . a cardboard valise." *Men I Hold Great*, trans. Elsie Pell (New York: Philosophical Library, 1951), pp. 124-5.

GRAHAM GREENE

97   "The Virgin. . . . furniture." *The Lawless Roads* (London: Heinemann, 1939), pp. 50-1.

      "the peasants. . . . heaven." *Roads*, pp. 44-5.

99   "The lieutenant. . . . them again." *The Power*, p. 32.

101   "It infuriated. . . . He knew." *The Power*, p. 33.

102   "She. . . . bonnet." *The Power*, p. 40.

103   "heard. . . . the corrupt." *The Power*, p. 131.

104   " 'He's dying. . . . both have.' " *The Power*, p. 239.

106   "God. . . . the priest." *The Power*, p. 136.

WILLIAM GOLDING

110   "was born . . . grab." *Pincher Martin* (New York: Harcourt Brace, 1956), p. 120.

112   "The Dean: 'Confess. . . . business.' " *The Spire* (New York: Harcourt, Brace, and World, 1964), pp. 38-40.

113   "The model. . . . new spire." *Spire*, p. 8.

      "My son. . . . to look at." *Spire*, p. 120.

114   "And the folly. . . . comes. *Spire*, p. 121.

115   "He saw one . . . . Dia Mater." *Spire*, pp. 79-80,

116   "What . . . . groundless spire." Wesley Kort, "The Groundless Glory of Golding's Spire" in *Renascence* 20:2 (winter 1968), pp. 77-8.

118   "We do not . . . actions." David Anderson, *The Tragic Protest* (London: SCM Press, 1969), p. 171.

MAUGHAM, LEWIS, AND DE VRIES

122   "You men! . . . Pig!" "Rain," *The Complete Short Stories of
W. Somerset Maugham*, vol. 1 (New York: Penguin Books, 1977),
p. 39.

123   "Mr. Carey. . . . the curate." *Of Human Bondage* (New York:
Garden City Publishing Company, 1939), p. 12.

"Oh William. . . . Sunday afternoon." *Bondage*, p. 13.

124   "Perhaps Religion. . . . behind." *Bondage*, p. 485.

128   "Jesus. . . . trolley on?" *The Mackerel Plaza* (Boston: Little,
Brown and Company, 1958), pp. 192-3.

129   "Oh, you're. . . . preacher. . . . Mister Mackerel." *Plaza*, p. 10.

"I believe. . . . their own." *Plaza*, p. 30.

FLANNERY O'CONNOR

135   "anagogical. . . ." "The Nature and Aim of Fiction," p. 72; "On Her
Own Work," p. 111; "Novelist and Believer," p. 159, in *Mystery and
Manners*, ed. Sally and Robert Fitzgerald (New York: Farrar, Straus,
& Giroux, 1969).

140   "good is . . . we see." "Catholic Novelists and Their Readers,"
Manners, p. 170.

149   "I have found . . . devil." "On Her Own Work," *Manners*, p. 118.

FREDERICK BUECHNER

151   "writing. . . . kind of sense." *Publisher's Weekly*, 29 March 1971,
p. 11.

157   "The tragic. . . . over them?" *Telling the Truth* (New York: Harper
& Row, 1977), p. 57.

"tales . . . best to be." *Truth*, p. 80.

"And the king. . . . everything." *Truth,* p. 90.

158   "In the world . . . Clergy. . . . anyone else!" *Truth*, p. 90.

160   "Antonio, I. . . . both of us." *Love Feast* (New York: Atheneum, 1974), p. 156.

"There are moments . . . a great banquet." *The Magnificent Defeat* (New York: The Seabury Press, 1968), pp. 87-8.

Cowley Publications is a work of the Society of St. John the Evangelist, a religious community for men in the Episcopal Church. The books we publish are a significant part of our ministry, together with the work of preaching, hospitality, and spiritual direction. Our aim is to provide books that will enrich their readers' religious experience as well as challenge it with fresh approaches to religious concerns.

M. Thomas Shaw, SSJE